GUIDE TO FRENCH INSTITUTIONS

by

J. Coveney, B.A.,
Docteur de l'Université de Strasbourg

and

S. Kempa, B.A.

Nelson

Thomas Nelson and Sons Ltd
Nelson House   Mayfield Road
Walton-on-Thames   Surrey
KT12 5PL   UK

51 York Place
Edinburgh
EH1 3JD   UK

Thomas Nelson (Hong Kong) Ltd
Toppan Building 10/F
22A Westlands Road
Quarry Bay   Hong Kong

Distributed in Australia by
Thomas Nelson Australia
480 La Trobe Street
Melbourne   Victoria 3000
and in Sydney, Brisbane, Adelaide and Perth

First published by Harrap Limited 1978
(under ISBN 0-245-532234)
Second impression published by Thomas Nelson and Sons
Ltd 1985

ISBN 0-17-444402-8
NPN 9 8 7 6

Printed in Hong Kong

PREFACE

As the title indicates, this work is not intended to be an exhaustive study of French institutions, but a guide to certain aspects which are frequently misunderstood on this side of the Channel. Comparisons are made, in passing, with corresponding British institutions in an attempt to emphasize differences and avoid facile identification.

Each chapter consists of a concise introduction to a particular sector, followed by a glossary in which we endeavour to explain, and in some cases find equivalents for, French specialised terms. The reader is assumed to have an adequate command of the French language, and terms easily found in dictionaries are, for the most part, omitted.

Descriptions of French political parties and a list of ministers are, for the reasons stated therein, dealt with in two appendices after the main body of the book.

Finally, we have included a list of abbreviations and acronyms which are commonly found in French books and journals, and which may present the British reader with some difficulty.

We would like to thank the Civil Service College, London, the Ecole Nationale d'Administration, Paris, and Monsieur R. Lejuez and Monsieur F. Marx of the French Embassy, London, for their helpful advice and suggestions.

J. COVENEY
S. KEMPA

CONTENTS

I THE LEGISLATURE

The Président de la République

The French head of State is the *Président de la République,* who is elected at seven-yearly intervals by a direct vote of the French electorate. The election is a *scrutin à deux tours* (two-ballot election) in the first stage of which all but the two most popular candidates are eliminated. The *Président de la République* is the administrative head of the nation, Commander in Chief of the armed forces, *Président du conseil des ministres,* and has the power to reprieve convicted criminals.

The French Parliament

France has a parliamentary system of government, the *Parlement* consisting of two chambers, the *Assemblée nationale* (lower chamber) and the *Sénat* (upper chamber). Both are elected bodies, although different forms of election are used for each.

The members of the *Assemblée nationale* are called *députés,* and they are elected by a direct vote of the electorate in a *scrutin à deux tours* which takes place every 5 years. The *circonscriptions électorales* (constituencies) are established by a process known as *découpage,* and in the case of the *élections législatives* (general elections) they do not correspond to any particular regional boundaries but are determined by the population of the area concerned. In order to win outright in the first stage of the election, a candidate must obtain an absolute majority of the votes cast and the votes of a quarter of the registered electorate. If no candidate succeeds in doing this a second ballot (called *ballottage*) is held in which only those candidates who have obtained at least 10% of the votes cast are eligible. In this ballot only a relative majority is required for a candidate to be elected.

The members of the *Sénat* are elected for a 9-year term, but every 3 years *élections sénatoriales* are held in which one third of the *sénateurs* are elected. They are not elected directly by the people but by the *députés* and the representatives of the *Conseils municipaux* and the *Conseils généraux* of each *département*. The elections take the form of a *scrutin de liste majoritaire,* or *scrutin plurinominal,* in which several candidates are elected by a majority of voters in a two-ballot election. The number of *sénateurs* in each *département* is determined by its population, and if 5 or more are to be elected a system of proportional representation is used instead.

Political parties

In France there are more political parties than in Britain, and more are represented in the *Parlement.* There have been attempts made over the last decade to reduce the number of parties represented in the two chambers by creating parliamentary alliances of parties with similar ideologies, thus facilitating the passing of new legislation.

Parliamentary groups

Within the *Parlement* the parties form larger groupings *(groupes parlementaires)* according to their general political tendencies, thus making it more difficult for small parties to block legislation. Each group must have a minimum of 30 members in the *Assemblée nationale* or 14 in the *Sénat,* and they must publish a manifesto of their political position. Some of the *députés* do not actually belong to a *groupe parlementaire,* but declare themselves in favour of one group's policies; these are called *apparentés.* There are also a few *députés* who do not subscribe to the policies of any of the groups; these are called the *non-inscrits.*

The Government

The body known as the *Gouvernement* consists of the *Premier ministre* (Prime Minister), the *ministres d'Etat* (Ministers of State), the *ministres* (ministers) and the *secrétaires d'Etat* (Secretaries of State). Its role is to ensure that legislation is properly executed and to formulate the general policy of the country. The leader of the Government is nominally the *Premier ministre,* but as both he and its other members are chosen by the *Président de la République,* it is in effect the *Président* who retains real control. The *Président de la République* is also the *Président du Conseil des ministres,* a body consisting of all the *ministres* and, under certain administrations, the *secrétaires d'Etat.* The *Conseil des ministres* meets regularly with the *Président de la République* in order to discuss and decide upon vital issues affecting the nation.

The *ministres* themselves, unlike their British counterparts, need not be chosen from among the ranks of parliamentary representatives. In fact, when a *député* is chosen to become a *ministre* he must resign his seat, which is then filled by a *suppléant* (substitute) elected at the same time in the *élections legislatives.*

The offices assigned to members of the Government vary from time to time, according to the needs of the country. The *Premier ministre* may at the same time hold another ministerial post, although when this happens another *ministre* or a *secrétaire d'Etat* is generally appointed to deal with the day-to-day running of the ministry concerned. The *ministres d'Etat* are senior members of the Government, but their title, while giving them a higher status, does not require them to undertake any additional duties.

The role of a minister is two-fold; he participates in the Government and its decision-making processes, and at the same time he is the head of a *département ministériel* or *ministère* (ministry), which is essentially an administrative structure. The minister is legally responsible for the actions of his department in the eyes of both private and administrative law (see Chapter VI).

Beneath the ministers in the hierarchy are the *secrétaires d'Etat,* most of whom are responsible for specific areas within the general scope of a ministry. There are, however, some *secrétaires d'Etat* who are not attached to a ministry but instead have other duties (e.g. *secrétaire d'Etat chargé des relations avec le Parlement*).

Conférence des présidents

In each of the two chambers the business of the day *(l'ordre du jour)* is decided by the *Conférence des présidents*. These two bodies consist of the *président* of the chamber, his *vice-présidents*, the *présidents* of both the permanent and special *commissions* (committees), the *présidents* of the parliamentary groups, the representative of the Finance Committee *(rapporteur général de la commission des finances)* and a representative of the Government *(ministre/secrétaire d'Etat chargé des relations avec le Parlement)*. Each assembly elects its *président* and *vice-présidents*.

Commissions parlementaires

The *Commissions parlementaires* are committees of varying size which discuss certain specific points of legislation in greater detail than is possible in the general session of the Parliament. There can be a maximum of six permanent *commissions* in each of the two chambers, as well as a number of *ad hoc* ones. Legislation is discussed by the *commissions* before it is passed to either the *Assemblée nationale* or the *Sénat* for debate.

Conseil économique et social

This body was set up in order to provide a medium through which experts in all fields can be consulted before a proposed law is discussed by Parliament. It has about 200 members who are drawn from various professions or groups with an interest in social and economic problems and who give their advice on how a proposed law will affect different sectors of the population.

Conseil d'Etat

This is a body consisting of about 200 experts in legal and administrative matters. It judges upon cases of administrative law and advises the *Parlement* on the legal aspects of proposed legislation.

Legislative procedure

The main function of the *Parlement* is to examine and approve new legislation. A *projet de loi* (bill proposed by the Government) or a *proposition de loi* (bill proposed by a private member) may be presented by any member of the two chambers. Theoretically any proposed law may be discussed first in either chamber, although Government proposals are usually examined first by the *Assemblée nationale*. The only exception to this is the annual *loi de finances,* the *projet* of which is always discussed first by the *Assemblée nationale*.

When a proposed law has been drawn up it goes to be examined first by the *Conseil économique et social*. In the case of proposals which affect national policy this examination is compulsory, but in other cases it is not. After this a *projet de loi* is studied by the *Conseil d'Etat* and then by the

Conseil des ministres, before going to be examined by one of the *commissions parlementaires.* A *proposition de loi* must be examined by a special committee *(délégation du bureau de l'Assemblée)* to see whether it is acceptable before it is passed to a *commission.* When it has been examined, printed and distributed to the members of the chamber in which it is to be presented, the proposed law can be put on the agenda for discussion. It is then given a first reading *(première lecture)* in that chamber where it may be passed as it stands, amended or rejected. It then goes to the other chamber, where it may also be approved, rejected or amended. It is passed between the two chambers until they both agree on all its details, this process being known as *la navette.* It is, however, possible to shorten the procedure if after two readings in each chamber no agreement has been reached, by setting up a *Commission mixte paritaire,* which is a committee consisting of seven representatives from each chamber, who try to find a compromise acceptable to both. If this also fails the *Assemblée nationale* has the power to make the final decision on the law.

When it has been agreed by both chambers the proposed law is sent to the Government and then to the *Conseil constitutionnel,* which checks that it conforms to the *Constitution.* After this it goes to the *Président de la République* for *promulgation,* the act which renders the law operative. It is then published in the *Journal officiel,* and this act of *publication* informs the public of the date on which the law comes into force, as well as setting it out in detail.

GLOSSARY

Action Française—a small right-wing political group which supports the French monarchy and various nationalistic ideals.

affaires courantes—the day-to-day administration of a nation.

alliance électorale—an alliance made for the purpose of winning an election between two or more groups that do not necessarily hold the same views.

arrêté—an official directive which may come from one of a number of bodies *(arrêté ministériel, municipal, préfectoral,* etc.).

assemblée constituante—an all-party body specially set up when it is necessary to make changes in the constitution.

assemblée consultative—any consultative body.

bicamérisme, bicaméralisme—a system of government in which the Parliament consists of two chambers.

bipartisme—a political system in which political power is effectively wielded by two parties. Two-party system.

campagne électorale—election campaign.

cautionnement électoral—deposit.

chambre—chamber, house (of Parliament).

Chef de l'Etat—Head of State. In France this is the *Président de la République.*

Chef du Gouvernement—Head of the Government. In France this is the *Premier ministre.*

circonscription électorale—electoral division, constituency. In elections for the *Sénat* the division is the *département,* while for municipal elections it is the *commune.* For the *élections législatives* the division is a specially created one (see text).

classe politique—those people who are involved in politics at a national or local level.

clubs—these are groups organised nationally or regionally, which discuss philosophical and political questions. They can play an influential role in forming a party's ideology.

comité électoral—people who help a candidate in an election. Campaign supporters.

commission—committee; commission. *Renvoyer un projet de loi en commission*—To refer a Bill to committee.

commission parlementaire—Parliamentary committee (see text).

conseil de cabinet—a meeting of all the members of the Government, including the *secrétaires d'Etat* and the *sous-secrétaires d'Etat*, with the *Premier ministre*.

Conseil constitutionnel—a body whose responsibility it is to ensure that the administration of the country is executed in a way that does not contravene the constitution.

Conseil interministériel (Comité interministériel)—a meeting of the highest ranking members of the ministries concerned in a specific issue. These are usually the *ministres,* the *secrétaires d'Etat* and the top civil servants. If the meeting is chaired by the *Président de la République* it is called a *Conseil interministériel*; if by the *Premier ministre* it becomes a *Comité interministériel.*

conseil restreint—an informal meeting between the *Président de la République* or the *Premier ministre* and members of the Government, at which some specific issue is discussed.

Constitution—France has a written constitution which can only be altered by a very complicated legal process. The last *Constitution* was drawn up in 1958 and modified in 1962.

contreseing ministériel—the signature of one or several senior Ministers on a document, witnessing and guaranteeing the signature of the *Président de la République.*

corps électoral—all the citizens of a country who have the right to vote. Electoral body.

Cour des comptes—the body which administers the finances of the country and regulates the accounts of all public organisations. Its decisions can be reversed only by the *Conseil d'Etat.*

débat parlementaire—Parliamentary debate.

déclaration du Gouvernement—official communiqué.

décret—a ruling by the *Président de la République* and the *Conseil des ministres* or by the *Premier ministre* on an administrative matter.

décret-loi—a legislative decision made by the Government and endorsed by the *Parlement,* taken as a temporary measure. Now replaced by the *ordonnance.*

département ministériel = *ministère*—ministry.

dépouillement—count (votes).

député—a member of the *Assemblée nationale* (see text).

désistement—after the first round of a *scrutin à deux tours* (see text), a candidate may be forced to retire, in which case he can advise his supporters to vote for another of the candidates. This is the act of *désistement.*

discipline parlementaire—Parliamentary discipline, requirement for members to obey the rule of procedure of their chamber.

discipline de vote—voting discipline, similar to the whip system in the British Parliament.

dissolution—dissolution. The French *Parlement* can be dissolved by the *Président* *de la République,* the *Premier ministre,* or by the *Parlement* itself.

district—an area of territory comprising several *communes.* Not often used.

droit d'amendement—the right to propose amendments to Bills. All members of the *Parlement* have this right, though not all to the same extent.

droit d'initiative—the right to present a Bill.

droit d'interpellation—the right to raise Parliamentary questions.

électeur—elector.

élection partielle—by-election.

électorat—electorate.

Elysée (Palais de l'E.)—the official residence of the *Président de la République.*

Front national—an extreme right-wing political group.

garantie des droits—the part of the French *Constitution* which provides for legislation guaranteeing the fundamental rights of the citizens.

Hôtel Matignon—the official residence of the *Premier ministre,* it also houses the *Secrétariat général du Gouvernement.*

incapacité électorale—ineligibility to vote through not fulfilling all the necessary conditions.

indemnité parlementaire—members' salary.

indignité électorale—ineligibility to vote as a result of a criminal conviction.

initiative gouvernementale—the Government's right to present a *projet de loi* to the *Parlement.*

initiative parlementaire—the right of *députés* and *sénateurs* to present a *proposition de loi* to the *Parlement.*

inscription électorale—electoral registration.

inviolabilité parlementaire—parliamentary immunity.

lecture—reading (of a Bill).

liste bloquée—in a *scrutin de liste* either the list is unchangeable *(liste bloquée),* or else the voter may be allowed to modify the order of the names or to add to or subtract from the list *(panachage).*

liste électorale—electoral register.

loi—law, Act of Parliament.

loi cadre—an Act which gives the general outline of a law, leaving the details to be filled in by one or more *décrets.*

loi constitutionnelle—an Act which modifies the constitution.

loi de finances—budget (see text).

loi de finances rectificative—"mini-budget".

loi d'habilitation—a law conferring a right or power to carry out an act (e.g. the right given to the Government to take legislative measures by means of an *ordonnance*).

loi ordinaire (loi parlementaire)—an Act concerned with a matter which is the sole responsibility of the *Parlement,* as defined in the constitution.

loi organique—an Act which clarifies a point of the constitution.

loi parlementaire—see *loi ordinaire.*

loi de programme—a five-year Government plan, which need not necessarily be carried out.

loi référendaire—an Act which is passed as a result of a referendum.

loi de règlement—an Act approving the State budget, and which is not debated.

maître de requêtes—member of the *Conseil d'Etat* whose duty is to present reports.

majorité—majority. The age of majority in France is now 18 years.

majorité parlementaire—parliamentary majority.

majorité présidentielle—those parliamentary groups which support the *Président de la République.* It is not necessarily the same as the *majorité parlementaire.*

mandat parlementaire—the right of an elected representative of the people to act on behalf of his electorate. Mandate.

marais électoral—a wavering between conservative and progressive policies.

multipartisme—a multi-party system of government, usually involving the creation of coalitions. It is the system used in France.

ordonnance—a legislative ruling made by the Government rather than by the *Parlement*. It becomes law only if ratified by the *Parlement*. The institution of the *ordonnance* has replaced that of the *décret-loi*.

ordre du jour—agenda; business of the day.

Palais Bourbon—the building in which the *Parlement* holds its debates.

panachage—see *liste bloquée*.

Plan de développement économique et social (le Plan)—a document drawn up by the *Commissariat général du plan d'équipement et de la productivité* and then passed by the *Parlement*, in which are laid out the steps that need to be taken in order to fulfil the economic and social policies of the Government. The *Plan* usually provides for measures extending over a period of three or four years.

Président de la République—President (see text).

questeur—in each of the two houses of the French *Parlement* there are three *questeurs*, whose duty it is to ensure that the premises which the house uses (apart from the chamber itself) are kept in good condition, and that the finances relating to the house are kept in order.

question d'actualité—Parliamentary question answered by either the *Premier ministre* or a minister.

question écrite—a written question which must be answered by the minister concerned in the *Journal officiel*.

questions au Gouvernement (questions du mercredi)—questions put to the Government.

question orale—an oral question to a minister. The matter may be debated or it may not, but if it is, no vote or resolution may be taken on it.

question préalable—a motion tabled before a debate in order to decide whether or not the debate will take place.

quotient électoral—in a system of proportional representation this is the minimum of votes which a candidate must receive in order to be elected.

rapporteur—a member of committee who is designated to report its proceedings to the rest of the chamber.

remaniement ministériel—"Government reshuffle".

représentativité—the legal right of some trade unions and other organisations to speak on behalf of their members.

réunion électorale—election meeting.

révision de la Constitution—the French *Constitution* can only be revised if a proposition from the *Premier ministre* and the *Parlement* is approved by the *Président de la République* and adopted by both chambers of the *Parlement*.

scrutin—vote; poll (see text).

secrétariat général du Gouvernement—this is a body consisting of about 25 officials, who are responsible for the secretarial and organisational aspects of ministerial meetings, such as the *Conseil des ministres*. Heading the service is the *secrétaire général du Gouvernement*, who is usually a member of the *Conseil d'Etat*.

secrétariat général de la Présidence de la République—this body acts in conjunction with the *secrétariat général du Gouvernement* in organising the *Conseil des ministres*. At the same time it keeps the *Président de la République* informed of activities inside the ministries and various other Governmental bodies.

sénateur—a member of the *Sénat*. Senator.

septennat—the seven-year period for which the *Président de la République* is elected.

suppléant—a person who is elected at the same time as a *député* so that, in the event of the death or promotion to ministerial duties of the *député*, a by-election would not need to be held. Substitute.

trésor public—a State-run service which administers public and some private finance. It is not the equivalent of the British Treasury, which has much wider powers.

vacances parlementaires—parliamentary recess.

vote bloqué—a method by which it is possible for the Government to require a chamber of the *Parlement* to vote on a Bill as it stands, without being able to amend it.

vote par correspondance—postal vote.

vote par procuration—vote by proxy.

II PUBLIC ADMINISTRATION

Public administration in France *(l'administration publique, la fonction publique)* is provided by a large and complex network of institutions, ranging from the Presidency through to local government. It can conveniently be divided into central administration, based in Paris with representatives in the provinces, and local administration, which employs people whose roots are in the area that they administer.

1. Central administration

Présidence de la République
This includes the *Président de la République* and his personal staff and is familiarly known as *"la maison"*. The President is the head of the executive and has the power effectively to choose its senior members.

Secrétariat général de la Présidence de la République
A body reponsible for planning and ordering the business of the *Conseil des ministres* and other meetings chaired by the President. It maintains the liaison between the President and the ministries, and at the same time carries out research for the preparation of various documents.

Cabinet du Président de la République
A group of personal advisors and aides to the President, chosen by him from any sector of employment.

Premier ministre
The *Premier ministre* is the *Chef du Gouvernement* and as such is the titular head of all the ministries. As it is the President, however, who chooses the *Premier ministre,* it is he who maintains effective control of the executive.

Cabinet du Premier Ministre
To help him perform his duties, the *Premier ministre* has a *cabinet* consisting of a number of advisers and experts of several types. Their function is to maintain the liaison between the *Premier ministre,* the *Présidence* and the various ministries. The members of this *cabinet* are chosen by the *Premier ministre* himself.

Secrétariat général du Gouvernement
This is a coordinating body with 25 members whose duty it is to prepare documents and arrange meetings for the *Conseil des ministres* and the

Conseil de cabinet, to obtain signatures from ministers and others as required, to work out timetables for the *Conseil des ministres* and generally to ensure that Government business runs efficiently.

Secrétariat général pour la Communauté et les affaires africaines et malgaches

This is a body which is responsible for maintaining the contact between the President and those countries which used to belong to the *Communauté,* various African countries and Madagascar. It also ensures that the aid and trading agreements with these countries are carried out correctly.

Ministères

It is in the *ministères* (ministries) that most of the decisions affecting the administration of the country are taken. At the head of each ministry is a *ministre* (minister), who is appointed by the *Premier ministre* with the approval of the President. The minister is aided by a *cabinet ministériel* (formerly known as a *cabinet du ministre*), which in theory is limited to about ten members, but which may in practice be considerably larger than this. The officially permitted posts in a *cabinet* are those of a *directeur* (who may be aided by an *adjoint*), a *chef du cabinet* and two *chefs-adjoints,* three *attachés,* a *chef de secrétariat* and two *chargés de mission* or *conseillers techniques.* These people are essentially experts in their own field, whose function is to advise the minister, but a number of them may have been appointed for political rather than professional reasons, although this practice is becoming less widespread than it used to be. They are all, however, known as *"officiels"* and their names are published in the *Journal officiel.* The *cabinet* also includes some members who are known as *"officieux",* because although they are full members of the *cabinet* and receive a salary, their names are not on the official list of members. In addition there may also be advisers in the *cabinet* whose names do not appear on any official list, who have no specific duties and who are not officially paid by the State, but who nevertheless play a very influential role in the *cabinet.* These people are known as *"clandestins",* and are often included in the *cabinet* for political reasons. All the members are appointed by the minister personally, and may also lose their places at his discretion. There is no British equivalent to the *cabinet ministériel,* and it is itself in no way comparable to the British Cabinet.

While the *cabinet ministériel* is a rather amorphous body, whose personnel is continually changing, the *bureau du ministère* constitutes a permanent and stable group of *fonctionnaires de carrière* (professional civil servants) who supervise the actual administrative work of the ministry. The *bureau* consists of *administrateurs civils, attachés d'administration* and *secrétaires d'administration,* who coordinate the work done by the various *directions.* An important but infrequent departmental office is that of the *secrétaire-général,* who is responsible for coordinating the activities of the *directions* and also those of the various ancillary services (public relations, post, research etc.).

Each *direction* (department) administers a particular area within the jurisdiction of the ministry. It is headed by a *directeur* or a *directeur-général* (who enjoys a higher status and salary than a *directeur,* but who does not necessarily have any more responsibility). The *directions* administer those areas for which the ministry is always responsible, but when a new Government policy comes into force this may necessitate the creation of a separate administrative division. In this case a *mission* is set up and a *chargé de mission* nominated to supervise it. The aim of *l'administration de mission* is to provide flexibility within the system, although many of the theoretically temporary *missions* eventually become permanent institutions.

The number of ministers varies from one government to another, and nearly all of them have a complete ministry beneath them. A ministry may also include one or more *Secrétariats d'Etat,* each of which is responsible for a major sub-section of the work of the ministry. In this case the organisation of the *Secrétariat* will be a microcosm of that of the ministry, and the *secrétaire d'Etat* will have his own personal *cabinet* to advise him. (See Chapter I.)

2 Local administration

To a much greater extent than in Britain decisions about local affairs are taken by a central authority, although there have recently been attempts made to remedy this by policies of *décentralisation,* involving the creation of regional elected bodies which have decision-making powers, and *déconcentration,* by means of which local representatives of central government have a certain amount of authority delegated to them.

Administration of the département

In every *département* in France there is a *préfet de département* who is the sole representative of the ministries. He is the only person to whom powers of decision may be delegated, although he in turn may delegate some of his authority to his *chefs de service.* The *préfet* is not elected but appointed to his post by the President and the *Conseil des ministres.* He is responsible for the execution of legislation within the *département,* and for the provision of information to the government. The *préfet de département* also has responsibility for the police force in *départements* where there is no *préfet de police,* i.e. in most cases.

The *préfet* attends, but does not chair, the meetings of the *Conseil général* in his *département.* This body consists of the elected representatives of each *canton,* and sits twice a year, once for up to 15 days and once for up to 30 days. Its function is to organise and administer public services and buildings, and to approve and keep a check on the budget for the *département,* which is drawn up by the *préfet.* It also gives its views on various matters to the *préfet,* who relays them to the Government, and it can intervene in matters relating to the *communes.* Finally, the *conseillers* take part in the election of senators.

As the *conseil général* meets only twice a year, another body is needed to take decisions at more frequent intervals and to ensure that the administration of the *département* is running smoothly. This body is the *commission départementale,* which consists of between 4 and 7 members elected for a year from the ranks of the *conseil général.* It gives its opinion on matters which will eventually be decided by the *conseil général,* and has some powers of decision itself in minor matters, but its main task lies in the execution of policies already made.

Administration of the commune

The 95 *départements* of metropolitan France are made up of 37,708 *communes,* which differ considerably in size of population. Each *commune* is administered by a *conseil municipal,* which consists of between 9 and 37 members depending on the size of the *commune* (except in the case of Paris, Lyons and Marseilles, which have a slightly modified system of local administration). The *conseil municipal* meets for 2 weeks four times a year and its main functions are to organise local public services, to manage public money and to be responsible for the registration of births, deaths and marriages.

When a *conseil municipal* has been elected it then proceeds to elect a *maire* and a number of *adjoints* (between 1 and 12, depending on the size of the *commune)* from amongst its own members. They, like the *conseil* itself, hold office for 6 years, or for the duration of the *conseil* if it is dissolved before that time has elapsed. The *maire* is at one and the same time a representative of the State like the *préfet* and a representative of the people, but, unlike the *préfet,* his main duty is towards the inhabitants of his *commune.* In his capacity as an agent of the State, the *maire* is responsible for the publication of official notices, organising elections and censuses, and for the supervision of the local police force.

3   Entry into French public administration

Entry into most grades of French public administration is generally through a *concours* (competitive examination), except for some clerical posts in which staff originally employed on a temporary basis are given permanent jobs. Having passed the examination, the civil servants then enter a *corps,* which is a grouping of all those people doing the same work (e.g. teachers, army officers, police commissioners). Each *corps* is subdivided and there are *échelons* (salary-steps) through which the civil servant passes as he is promoted. Promotion is almost exclusively determined by seniority, which makes for a large amount of rigidity within the system.

Ecole nationale d'administration (ENA)

Founded in 1945, with a view to democratising entry into the upper grades of French public administration, the ENA today is the starting point for many high-ranking civil servants. Entry into the ENA is by one of two extremely competitive examinations, one open to university graduates in appropriate subjects, the other open to existing civil servants. Despite its intentions, the ENA's intake is still drawn overwhelmingly from the Parisian upper middle class, and its existence seems only to have reinforced the élitist tendencies of the administration's recruitment policies. The course of study consists of subjects relevant to the work of a senior administrator interspersed with some very demanding examinations, and includes a period of time usually spent working in a *préfecture* away from Paris. At the end of the course, posts in the administration are allotted according to the examination results, with the most coveted posts in the *Grands corps* going to those with the best results.

GLOSSARY

acte administratif—this can take the form of a *décret*, an *arrêté*, an *ordonnance*, or a *décision*, and constitutes an administrative ruling carrying the force of law, but which does not need to go through the usual legislative procedures. It must, however, conform to an already existing legal framework, e.g. planning permission, compulsory purchase.

activité: être en situation d'a.—to be on the active list.

adjudication—see *marché public*.

administrateurs civils: corps des a.c.—this *corps*, instituted in 1945, was designed to break down some of the barriers between the ministries, which have traditionally operated in virtual isolation from each other. Previously, the career structure of each ministry was such that a civil servant could not transfer from one ministry to another without hindering his promotion prospects, but the *administrateurs civils*, in theory at least, can be sent to work in any ministry. They are selected for the most part from graduates of the ENA.

administration active—this is the section of the administration which executes policies which have been elaborated by others, as opposed to *l'administration consultative*, which is the section where discussion and investigation take place and decisions are finally made.

administration centrale—this term refers to those services which are directly linked to the Government in Paris, as opposed to the *services extérieurs*, which represent the Government in the provinces. Central offices.

administration consultative—see *administration active*.

administration locale—a general term for all public administration outside the central offices.

administré—this refers to any private person who is in a legal relationship to the administration, i.e. all French citizens, as the state of citizenship involves such a relationship.

affectation: lieu d'a.—appointment; place of employment.

agents diplomatiques—diplomatic staff.

agents publics—all those people who work in the public sector. Public employees.

aménagement du territoire—a term used to describe the economic and spatial reorganisation of France's territorial resources. Regional planning and land-use.

ampliation—a signed, authenticated copy of an administrative ruling.

appel d'offres—see *marché public*.

arrêt—a term used to describe a decision made by the *Conseil d'Etat*.

arrêté—an administrative ruling made by an authority invested with the appropriate power. (See text.)

arrondissement—an administrative division, of which there are between 2 and 6 in each *département,* responsibility for which is in the hands of a *sous-préfet.* (In Paris, Lyons and Marseilles, however, the term refers to a subdivision of the *commune* itself.)

attachés d'administration—these are civil servants whose job it is to do the routine work for the *administrateurs civils.* Unlike the latter, they are attached to particular ministries, although their conditions of employment are laid down on an interministerial basis.

auxiliaire—an employee in public administration who does not enjoy the status (legal status, guaranteed employment, career structure, etc.) given to the *fonctionnaire* proper. They are often found in the lower clerical ranks of the hierarchy, but the largest single group of them is that of the *maîtres auxiliaires* in secondary schools. (See *non-titulaires.*)

avancement—this can take the form of *avancement d'échelon* (increment), where the employee receives an increase in salary, or *avancement de grade* (promotion), where the employee receives new status and responsibilities.

canton—an electoral division consisting of up to about 30 *communes.*

catégorie—French civil servants are divided into four *catégories,* A, B, C and D, as far as salary and responsibilities are concerned, with 'A' corresponding to the group of senior civil servants. Within each *catégorie* there are many different *grades* (offices), which are denoted by their respective titles, and to which the employee is promoted for merit or for long service. Each *grade* consists of several *échelons,* which are steps in the salary scale and are awarded automatically.

Centre de préparation à l'administration générale (CPAG)—a type of educational establishment under the authority of the *Ministère de l'éducation* for training prospective civil servants for the entrance examinations of the various ministries.

Commissariat général du Plan—an institution created in 1946 in order to coordinate the execution of different parts of the *Plan de développement économique et social.*

Commission centrale des marchés de l'Etat (CCME)—a body which coordinates the activities of the seven consultative committees responsible for tenders, contracts and buying from private firms on behalf of public bodies.

Communauté—this was originally a grouping of France's colonies giving them each a certain amount of autonomy within the framework of government from France. However, as many of these colonies have since become independent states, the *Communauté conventionnelle* (as it is now called) serves as a cultural and economic link between those countries and France.

commune—this is the smallest territorial division in France and constitutes the basic unit for both administrative and electoral purposes.

comptabilité publique—this term is used to indicate the many rules and regulations surrounding public expenditure and income.

concertation—a type of "in-depth" consultation, used mainly in the drawing-up of economic, political and regional policies.

conseil régional—a body that decides on policy with a *région,* of which at least 30% must be made up of representatives of the *communes,* elected by members of the *conseils généraux.* The other members of the *conseil régional* are the *députés* and *sénateurs* for that *région,* and representatives of its urban areas.

Conseil supérieur de la fonction publique—this is a consultative and coordinating body which is mostly concerned with the conditions of employment applying to civil servants. It is made up of 32 members who are chosen by the *Conseil des ministres* (although half the names are proposed by the relevant *syndicats* and half are representatives of the administration). The members hold office for a period of three years.

contractuels—these are people employed by the administration at all levels, but who differ from the *fonctionnaire* inasmuch as they do not benefit from the guarantees of employment, career structure, etc. that fully established *fonctionnaires* enjoy, but are merely under contract to the administration. (See *non-titulaires*).

contrat administratif—a type of contract used in certain specific types of agreement in which one party is the administration (e.g. public works, sale of State property). It differs from a normal contract in that it gives the administration an unusual amount of control over the manner in which the work is carried out.

département—1. A *département ministériel* or ministry. 2. An administrative division. France is divided into 95 *départements* plus the four *Départements d'outre-mer* (Guyane, Guadeloupe, Martinique and Réunion), which have a special status.

dérogation—an act by which a particular case is made the exception to a general rule, e.g. the granting of planning permission for a building which does not conform to the planning regulations for the area.

détachement—the state of a civil servant who has been seconded to a post outside the administration. He remains a member of his *corps* and continues to progress with regard to pension and promotion rights, but no longer receives his salary from the administration.

directeur adjoint; adjoint au directeur; sous-directeur—the *directeur adjoint* and the *sous-directeur* do broadly similar work in assisting the *directeur,* although the former position usually carries a higher status. The title of *adjoint au directeur* is an unofficial one, generally given to someone who is about to become a *directeur adjoint*.

disponibilité—the state of a civil servant who has temporarily left his *corps.* In this case he loses not only his salary, but also his pension and promotion rights.

droit administratif—a very important difference between the British and French concepts of public administration is that in France the administration is not subject to ordinary civil law, but to a special system of administrative law which seeks to separate completely the judiciary from the administration, thus ensuring the independence of the latter. (See Chapter VI.)

échelon—see *catégorie* and text.

emploi réservé—a certain number of administrative posts are always reserved for some military personnel no longer on active service, war victims, widows and orphans, and other handicapped people.

établissement public—a public service (e.g. hospitals, universities, chambers of commerce) which has a budget separate from that of the State, and which constitutes a legal person in its own right.

expropriation indirecte—compulsory purchase.

fisc—the part of the administration responsible for taxes.

fonction publique—civil service.

grade—see *catégorie*.

Grands corps—this term is used to describe the most prestigious sections of the French administration. It usually refers to the *Conseil d'Etat,* the *Cour des comptes* and the *Inspection générale des finances,* but by extension it can also include the *Corps diplomatique* and the *Corps préfectoral,* as well as some of the technical *corps.*

gré à gré—see *marché public*.

huissier—usher (in a ministry).

Imprimerie nationale—the equivalent of HMSO.

Inspecteur général de l'économie nationale (IGEN)—an official who acts as a link between the Government and the *préfet de région* with regard to economic policy.

Inspection générale des finances (IGF)—one of the *Grands corps*, this body is ultimately responsible for the financial administration of public money from all sources. In addition, many important posts in various ministries, as well as in nationalised banks and industries, are held by members of this *corps*.

Instituts régionaux d'administration (IRA)—training establishments for newly recruited civil servants of *catégorie A*.

Journal officiel (JO)—see Chapter I. The *Journal officiel* comes under the auspices of the *services du Premier ministre*, and not those of the *Imprimerie nationale*.

Légion d'honneur (Ordre de la L.d'h.)—the highest civil decoration, awarded for long and meritorious public service, for the most part to higher civil servants.

lettres de créance/de provision—documents proving that a diplomat is an official representative of his Government, which are handed over to the Head of State or Minister of Foreign Affairs of the country to which the diplomat has been sent. In the case of Consuls the documents are called *lettres de provision*.

maître d'œuvre—a person who supervises and coordinates building or buying operations in the public sector which have been ordered by a *maître d'ouvrage*. This latter takes on the financial and decision-making responsibilities, and can be a local authority, a ministry or any other public body.

maître d'ouvrage—see *maître d'œuvre*.

marché public—this term refers to a contract between a public body and a private business which undertakes to carry out work or supply goods for the former. Contracts can be awarded by one of three procedures: 1. *adjudication*; the contract is offered to any interested firm and awarded to the lowest tender. 2. *appel d'offres*; the contract is offered publicly *(appel d'offres ouverts)* or to firms chosen by the public body *(appel d'offres restreints)*, and awarded to a firm chosen by the public body, not necessarily the lowest bidder. 3. *gré à gré*—the contract is awarded to a firm chosen by the public body without any invitation to tender.

maroquin—a familiar term referring to the ministerial portfolio.

médiateur—a person chosen by the Government, holding office for 6 years, who is responsible for investigating complaints made by the public about the administrative machinery of the country.

mutation—a change of post for a civil servant on the orders of his superiors. Transfer.

non-titulaires—these are people who work for the State but who do not enjoy the status and privileges of the *fonctionnaire titulaire* (established civil servant). They fall into one of three categories, *auxiliaires*, *contractuels* and *vacataires*, and form nearly a third of all public employees in France.

notation—a type of yearly report made on each civil servant by his head of department so that his suitability for promotion can be assessed.

ouvrier d'Etat—this status is held by a number of workers in some particular branches of the public sector (e.g. *service des postes et télécommunications*) but not by workers in nationalised industries and businesses.

pantouflage—a familiar term used to describe the act (usually by a higher civil servant) of leaving public service to take up a post in the private sector.

police nationale—the French police force is divided into five sections, the largest of which is the *police urbaine* or *gardiens de la paix*, who are responsible for keeping the peace in towns and public highways. The *Compagnies républicaines de sécurité (CRS)* form a branch which backs up the *police urbaine* if the need arises, being specially trained in riot control. Two other branches are the *Renseignements généraux (RG)*, which deal with political matters and police the national frontiers, and the *Direction de la surveillance du territoire (DST)*, which is responsible for State security and counter-espionage. Finally, the *police judiciaire* is responsible for bringing criminals and other law-breakers to justice. In addition to the police force, there is also the *gendarmerie nationale*, controlled by the *Ministère de la defense*, which performs policing functions on the departmental and regional levels, but which is essentially a military force.

région—France is divided into 20 *régions*, which form a new type of administrative division with as yet only vaguely defined competences. Each *région* is the responsibility of a *préfet de région*, who is also the *préfet* of one of the *départements* contained within the *région*.

règlement—this is a general term for an administrative ruling or regulation, which may take the form of a *décret, arrêté*, etc. Unlike a *loi* it does not need to be passed by the *Parlement*; it can, however, be contested in the law courts, which a *loi* cannot. A *décret* from the *Conseil d'Etat*, made to facilitate the application of a *loi*, is known as a *règlement d'administration publique*.

sanction administrative—the administration has the power to impose certain sanctions without going through the law courts, e.g. suspension of driving licence, various punishments which can be applied to financial defrauders.

secrétaire général de ministre—this post (which is essentially one of coordination) exists in only a few ministries and constitutes the highest authority after that of the *ministre*. There is, therefore, often an overlapping of the functions of the *secrétaire général* and the *cabinet*, which has led to the gradual decline of the former institution.

secrétaire général de préfecture—an offical who coordinates the activities of the various internal services provided by the *préfecture*.

secrétaire particulier—private secretary; personal assistant.

secrétariat général de préfecture—the department of the *secrétaire général de préfecture*.

services extérieurs—these are local sections of certain branches of administration, and not part of the ministries themselves. They have a measure of decision-making power and are a sign of the move towards *déconcentration*.

statut général des fonctionnaires (SGF)—this is a text which lays down the general conditions of employment of civil servants in France, as well as the special privileges and responsibilities they hold.

titulaire (fonctionnaire t.)—established civil servant.

tribunal administratif—a law court which hears the preliminary stages of any matter that comes under the jurisdiction of administrative law. (See Chapter VI.)

vacataire—a person who works for the administration on an irregular basis and who does not enjoy the special status of a *fonctionnaire*. (See *non-titulaires*.)

III INDUSTRY AND COMMERCE

Monopolies

French companies are typically either gigantic, impersonal organisations or small family firms, with relatively little in between, despite the Government's (somewhat unsuccessful) attempts to encourage mergers in the national interest. Monopolies or oligopolies are not frowned upon, so long as they benefit the country's economy, although the *Commission technique des ententes et positions dominantes* and the *Office de contrôle des monopoles privés* exist to prevent large firms from abusing their position in the market. Some monopolies are state-owned, for example the *Société nationale des chemins de fer français (SNCF)*, whilst others are privately owned.

Public Ownership

The degree of public control of industry is rather greater in France than in Britain and has been increasing steadily since the end of the Second World War. Publicly-owned concerns can be divided roughly into three types:
  i) Public services financed directly from the national budget (e.g. *service des postes et télécommunications*), and services (usually known as *régies*) provided by local authorities (e.g. transport).
 ii) Companies of a commercial or industrial nature whose capital is wholly State-owned, but which are nevertheless subject to the same laws as private businesses and may be in competition with them. Some have been specially created by the State while others are the result of a State take-over of a formerly private concern. Some major examples are: *Charbonnages de France, Compagnie nationale du Rhône, Electricité de France, Gaz de France, Régie Renault.*
iii) *Sociétés d'économie mixte*—These are either self-financing branches of publicly-owned firms, or private firms in which 30% or more of the shares are owned by public bodies. This is an extremely flexible type of organisation which makes it very popular in the field of public amenities. Some examples of this type of company are: *Air France, Air Inter, Compagnie des messageries maritimes, Compagnie française des pétroles, Société nationale des chemins de fer français, ELF/ERAP, Société nationale industrielle aérospatiale, Caisse nationale du crédit agricole,* etc.

Private businesses

Privately-owned firms can, as in Britain, take one of several legal forms, depending on the size and aims of the business. The smallest type is the *entreprise individuelle* (one-man business), in which the owner not only provides most if not all of the capital, but also performs all the functions of management and some or even all of those of worker. If he employs additional labour, the business becomes an *entreprise individuelle différenciée*. Although many small concerns have been put out of business with the growth of large national and international companies, they still play a much more significant part in the economic and social life of France than do their British counterparts.

Somewhat larger than the *entreprise individuelle* is the *société des personnes*, which corresponds to the British partnership. The *associés* (partners) provide the capital and have an unlimited responsibility for any debts that the business may incur.

For medium-sized firms the most usual type of organisation is the *société à responsabilité limitée (SARL)*, which is the equivalent of the British private company. The associates, who must number between 2 and 50, provide a fully paid-up capital sum, the minimum amount of which is laid down by law. The company does not issue shares and the ownership of a "stake" in the company may not be freely transferred. The associates are only liable for the company's debts up to the amount of the capital they have provided.

For large companies the most practical form of organisation is the *société anonyme (SA)*, which like the British limited company offers shares for sale to the general public. The shares are freely negotiable, and the shareholders, of whom there must be at least 7, are liable for the company's debts only up to the value of their shares.

There are also other types of business which fulfil specific needs. One is the *association commerciale en participation*, in which the names of the associates are not published. Another is the *société à capital variable*, in which the amount of capital can be increased easily by the introduction of new associates. This type of business forms the legal basis for cooperatives, which play an essential role in French agriculture.

Internal organisation of companies

There are two types of *société anonyme*: the *type classique* and the *type nouveau*. The *type classique* has at its head a *conseil d'administration* (board of directors) with between three and twelve members, one of whom is elected by the others to be its *président* (chairman). He may also perform the functions of managing director, in which case he is known as a *président directeur général (PDG)*. Other members of the *conseil* are the *administrateur directeur général* (managing director) and the *administrateurs* (directors).

In 1966 a law was passed enabling companies, if they wished, to form companies of the "type nouveau". In this kind of organisation the *conseil d'administration* is replaced by two bodies each with its own chairman.

They are the *conseil de surveillance,* which is responsible for the financial and legal affairs of the company, and the *directoire,* which is responsible for the actual day-to-day management of the firm.

Further down the hierarchy posts vary according to the size and nature of the company. The *directeur général* (general manager) supervises the day-to-day running of the firm. Financial matters are dealt with by the *trésorier* (chief accountant). In the case of a *société anonyme* the account books must be inspected periodically by the *Commissaire aux comptes,* who is a Government auditor.

Worker representation in management

If a company has more than 50 employees on its payroll a *comité d'entreprise* (works council) must be set up to advise on labour and economic questions. The *comité* consists of the employer (or his delegate) and workers' delegates elected every 2 years from candidates nominated by the *syndicats.*

In any firm with more than 10 employees the staff are also represented by the *délégués du personnel* who are elected by a vote in which all the employees take part. Their role is to advise on matters relating to conditions of employment and, if need be, to report any complaints to the *Inspection du travail.*

GLOSSARY

Accord général sur les tarifs douaniers et le commerce—General Agreement on Tariffs and Trade (GATT).

accord type—standard contract.

Agence nationale pour l'emploi—A State-run employment service, similar to the British Job Centres.

Association européenne de libre-échange (AELE)—European Free-Trade Association. (EFTA).

Association française pour l'étiquetage d'information (AFEI)—a body which, in conjunction with the *Conseil national du patronat français* is engaged in persuading manufacturers to label their products truthfully and usefully.

Association française de normalisation (AFNOR)—a body which lays down standards to which products of many types should conform. Products which do conform to these specifications may bear the *marque NF,* similar to the British Standards "kite-mark".

Bureau international du travail (BIT)—International Labour Office (ILO).

chambres de commerce et de l'industrie—public bodies, of which there is at least one in every *département,* set up to defend the interests of businessmen and industrialists, whose representatives form the membership of the bodies.

Chambre de commerce internationale (CCI)—International Chamber of Commerce (ICC).

Comité économique et social—Economic and Social Committee. A European Communities advisory body consisting of representatives of the member States of the Communities, of which a third represent employers, a third employees and a third economic specialists.

Comité consultatif en matière d'ententes et de positions dominantes—a public body set up to prevent abuse of the monopoly held by some firms and to ensure that no trading agreements are made against the public interest. Similar to the British Monopolies Commission.

Communauté économique européenne (CEE)—European Economic Community (EEC).

Conseil de coopération douanière—Customs Cooperation Council.

Conseil économique et social—a body which advises the French Government on economic and social policy matters.

démarchage à domicile—door-to-door selling.

établissements publics—these are bodies which either (a) provide a public service or (b) constitute a commercial entity but are publicly owned.

établissements d'utilité publique—this designation is given to certain privately-owned organisations which nevertheless benefit the public.

Fonds de développement économique et social (FDES)—part of the budget of the *Trésor*, it provides loans for economic and social development as laid down in the *Plan*.

impôt—a generalised tax levied in order to provide money for public services (see *taxe*).

Inspection du travail—part of the French public administration responsible for seeing that laws about work and employment are respected, similar to the British Factory Inspectorate.

Institut national de la propriété industrielle (INPI)—a Government body which investigates and grants patents for inventions, similar to the British Patents Office. It also keeps a register of trade-marks.

label—a type of trade mark guaranteeing that the product has been manufactured under certain conditions.

Marché commun—Common Market.

Office de contrôle des monopoles privés—a Government body which regulates the activities of private monopolies, i.e. monopolies which exist and have received official sanction.

Offre publique d'achat (OPA)—this procedure must be carried out if a person or company is planning to take a controlling interest in the shares of another company, so that the other shareholders know about the takeover. It consists of informing the shareholders concerned that the person or company is prepared to acquire their shares at a specific price.

Organisation de coopération et de développement économiques (OCDE)—Organisation for Economic Cooperation and Development (OECD).

Organisation international du travail (OIT)—International Labour Organisation (ILO).

patronat—a general term for all employers.

président—chairman (of a company).

président directeur-général (PDG)—chairman and managing director, executive chairman.

salariat—a general term for all employees.

société d'économie mixte—semi-public company (see text).

tantièmes—share of the profits.

taxe—a type of tax or duty levied for a specific service such as the issuing of a marriage certificate (see *impôt*).

taxe sur la valeur ajoutée (TVA)—Value Added Tax.

trésorier-payeur général—an official of the *Cour des comptes*, the *trésorier-payeur général* acts as the chief auditor in each *département* of France and is solely responsible for ensuring that public money is properly accounted for, and that the requisite receipts and payments are made.

IV INDUSTRIAL RELATIONS

Union Organisations

The basic unit of the union movement in France is the *syndicat,* which may represent the workers of an industry (e.g. metalworkers), a grade in the hierarchy (e.g. technicians) or a trade, although this last type of grouping seems to be very much on the decline. Generally speaking, the local *syndicat* does not represent the workers of a single firm, except in the situation where a large firm dominates the employment of a particular locality, when the *section* at that works will probably constitute the whole of the local branch. In many cases, therefore, the representative of the *syndicat* in an industrial dispute will not be a worker in the firm concerned, nor even, perhaps, practise the same trade as the workers he represents. The *unions départementales* (see below) play an important role in organising and coordinating any action, especially when the local branch of the *syndicat* is weak.

The national confederations, the three largest of which are the CGT, the CFDT and the FO, are coordinating bodies, each composed of two different types of smaller group, the *fédérations d'industrie* and the *unions locales, départementales et régionales.* The former bring together on a national level *syndicats* representing workers in a single industry, while the latter are regional, departmental and local associations of *syndicats* representing different industries, and may be compared with the British Trades Councils. The confederations, because of their conflicting political leanings, seldom agree with each other over a particular issue, and this divergence constitutes one of the major weaknesses of the French movement. They can in no way be compared to the British TUC, for which no French equivalent exists.

On the shop-floor the *syndicat* is not an integral part of day-to-day life as is the union in many British industries, but instead it is the concern of a handful of dedicated *syndicalistes* who spend much of their time attempting to collect subscriptions from members. Membership is, in any case, neither constant nor to be relied upon, as it fluctuates according to the prevailing political and economic climate. The membership figures are never known exactly because the *syndicats* are unwilling to disclose them and also because members tend to drop out during the course of a year. In this situation there can obviously be no equivalent of the closed shop or union shop found in Britain.

The low membership levels and inadequate subscription rates mean that the funds held by the *syndicat* are usually rather meagre, if they are not actually in the red. Administrative costs are high, and union funds are often voted to worthy political causes, with the result that strike funds, when they exist at all, are insufficient to sustain the type of long-term strike which is a feature of the British trades unions. In the event of a long-running strike money is obtained by appeals to sympathetic organisations and the general public, which does more to gain popular support than to impress the employers with the union's power.

In the event of an industrial dispute the *inspecteur du travail* is called in to arbitrate and the decision is taken out of the hands of the interested parties. After discussion the employers and representatives of the various unions involved may draw up a *convention collective* to fix rates of pay or working conditions. In the last resort the workers may call a strike.

The long-term strike or *grève illimitée* is the least frequent type of strike in France. More usual is the *arrêt de travail* (also called *grève*) which has a time-limit set on it. The *grève tournante* is a strike which affects different parts of a plant in rotation. The *grève perlée* involves a slowing-down of production, usually by refusal to work overtime. The *grève surprise* (wildcat strike) and *grève sur le tas* (down-tools) are strikes which have not been announced in advance. The *grève du zèle* (work-to-rule) requires workers, usually in service industries, to obey the rules of their job down to the last letter, thus causing long delays. Finally the *grève sauvage*, or unofficial strike, is not a feature of French industrial life if only because virtually all strikes are organised at a local level and are not required to have the approval of the movement as a whole.

Employers' organisations

Employers in France, like those in Britain, are organised both on a local and on a national scale. The *Conseil national du patronat français (CNPF)* is a confederation of smaller groups representing employers of all types, in many ways comparable with the Confederation of British Industry. Some of its most influential member groups are the *Union des industries métallurgiques et minières (UIMM)*, the CGPME and the CFPC (see below). Its constituent bodies, like those of the CGT, represent two types of grouping: the "vertical" federations of producers of similar products, and the "horizontal" associations of employers within a region. In the case of the CNPF, however, it is the former which are the more important.

Within the CNPF it is the federations of manufacturing industries which have the most influence (and also, incidentally, make the largest contributions to its funds), but there are other groups which should not be overlooked. The small business still plays a much more important part in the French economy than it does in the British, and for this reason the *Confédération générale des petites et moyennes entreprises*, representing small businessmen and shopkeepers, is a powerful pressure group. The CGPME is a vociferous organisation, acting to a great extent indepen-. dently of the CNPF, while remaining a member of it. Unlike the other employers' federations, the CGPME frequently puts its case before the public by means of demonstrations, refusal to pay taxes, and even shopkeepers' strikes.

There are other organisations, less influential than the CGPME, which also represent the small businessman. Two of these are the *Centre français du patronat chrétien* (also known as the *Confédération française des professions*) and the *Centre des jeunes patrons,* both of which are primarily Catholic in leaning, although the latter does not actually incorporate Catholic principles into its statutes.

Neither of these organisations is particularly influential, unlike the *Association des cadres dirigeants de l'industrie* (ACADI), which represents directors of industrial firms. Its members are coopted, thus keeping the association tightly-knit and stable. ACADI, through its network of study groups, provides much important economic information about both the public and the private sectors of industry.

The function of the CNPF is primarily to coordinate the activities of its members rather than to dictate to them. By means of an extremely flexible system of sub-committees it is able to identify and study many of the problems associated with industry and commerce at all levels. Not only the large manufacturing industries, but the whole range of commercial enterprises right down to the small shopkeeper are represented in fair proportion to their numerical strength, so that the interests of the CNPF are by no means limited to those of the industrial giants. Both social and economic questions are within its frame of reference, and in this respect it resembles its British equivalent, the CBI.

In the event of an industrial dispute the role of the CNPF is purely advisory; no decision that it makes is binding on any of its members, nor does it have any power to negotiate on their behalf, since the real decisions will in any case be taken at Governmental level. Nevertheless, it is able to put the employers' case to the Government, which it can usually do very convincingly thanks to the information and statistics supplied by its sub-committees.

GLOSSARY

arrêt de travail—strike, stoppage, "industrial action".

autogestion—workers' control. Advocated by some unions, principally the CFDT.

chômage—unemployment.

Confédération française démocratique du travail (CFDT)—the second largest union organisation in France, drawing its membership mainly from industry, although it has some influence among white-collar workers. Its policies are socialist, and it is in favour of workers' control of industry.

Confédération française des travailleurs chrétiens (CFTC)—the fourth largest union organisation in France, it draws its membership from employees of all types and incorporates Christian (mainly Catholic) values into its policies.

Confédération générale des cadres (CGC)—a union organisation representing executive and managerial staff in the private sector.

Confédération générale du travail (CGT)—the largest union organisation in France, drawing its membership mainly from the large industries, especially the nationalised ones. Its political orientation is towards the French Communist Party.

Confédération générale du travail—Force ouvrière (CGT-FO)—see *Force ouvrière.*

Conseil national du commerce (CNC)—an employers' organisation operating within the framework of the CNPF.

convention collective—an agreement about terms of employment drawn up between employers and union organisations.

droit syndical—the right to organise; trade union law.

Fédération de l'éducation nationale (FEN)—a federation of the main union organisations representing teachers and lecturers. Within it there are two political leanings, one socialist, the other communist.

Fédération nationale des syndicats d'exploitants agricoles (FNSEA)—the main union organisation representing farmers. It is Christian Democrat in its political leaning.

fédérations d'industrie—federations of trade unions representing workers in a single industry.

Force ouvrière (FO)—the third largest union organisation in France, representing white collar workers in the civil service and elsewhere, as well as other workers from various industries. It is socialist in its political leaning.

formation continue/permanente—covers various schemes for improving the skills of workers and professional people who have finished their formal training.

grève—strike, "industrial action". (For different types, see text.)

inspecteur du travail—a civil servant whose job it is to ensure that the conditions of employment are satisfactory to both employer and employee and that agreements are being adhered to by both parties (see text).

paritaire (adj.)—a *discussion paritaire* is one in which both sides are equally represented.

permanents (n.)—full-time union officials.

poujadisme—in a general sense, a conservative movement which defends the interests of small businessmen, craftsmen and consumers, named after Pierre Poujade, who inspired it.

Salaire minimum de croissance (SMIC)—the minimum hourly rate that any worker can be paid. It is linked to the cost of living index and to a national index of wage levels and may be revised several times a year, as the need arises.

Salaire minimum interprofessionnel garanti (SMIG)—an hourly minimum rate of pay, replaced in 1970 by the SMIC.

section—the smallest grouping of unionists, representing workers in one town or small area. Branch.

V BANKING

The Banque de France

The central pivot of the French banking system is the *Banque de France* which, like the Bank of England, functions as banker for the State, through the *Trésorerie,* as the sole note-issuing authority in France, as banker for the other banks and as regulator of the interest and exchange rates on the money market. It is entirely state-owned and is headed by a Governor and two Deputy Governors who are chosen by the *Conseil des ministres.* Its commercial transactions are now so few as to be negligible.

Commercial Banks

There are two types of bank which fulfil the usual banking functions of holding deposits, granting loans and performing other commercial services. These are the *banques de dépôts* and the *banques d'affaires,* but since the reforms of 1966 their fields of operation have overlapped to such an extent that the only apparent major difference between them is the scale of their involvement in business concerns. The *banques de dépôts* are not allowed to hold more than 20% of the capital of private firms.

The three largest *banques de dépôt* are the *Banque nationale de Paris,* the *Crédit lyonnais* and the *Société générale,* which are all publicly owned. They compete for custom on equal terms with the privately-owned deposit banks, some of which are subsidiaries of leading merchant banks. There are over 300 registered banks in France, of which about 250 are French, compared to 55 members of the British Bankers Association, 22 of which are domestic British banks.

Credit Banks

In addition to the commercial banks there are a number of establishments dealing in long- and medium-term loans, the *banques de crédit à long et moyen terme.* These are publicly owned and fall into two groups, the first of which consists of the *Crédit agricole* and the *Crédit populaire,* which both collect deposits and make loans to finance agriculture and small businesses respectively. They are based on a network of small local banks and have a cooperative-type membership.

The second group is made up of a number of other establishments such as the *Crédit foncier,* the *Crédit national* and the *Caisse des dépôts et consignations,* which loan money to both public and private bodies for specialised purposes like house-building, financing exports and investment in industry.

It is worth noting that there is no French equivalent of the British building society; loans for buying property must be obtained through the banks.

There are, however, significantly fewer owner-occupiers of houses in France than in Britain.

Savings banks

Small savers are served by the *caisses d'épargne* (savings banks), of which there are two kinds. The first type are privately-owned but designated as being in the public interest, and are supervised by the *Ministère de l'économie*. In addition there is the *Caisse nationale d'épargne*, which is run by the *service des postes et télécommunications*. These two types of bank are equivalent to the British Trustee Savings Banks and the Post Office Savings Bank.

GLOSSARY

acompte—payment on account.
banque d'affaires—merchant bank (see text).
banque de crédit à long et moyen terme—long- and medium-term credit bank (see text).
banque de dépôt—deposit bank (see text).
Banque européenne d'investissements (BEI)—a bank which makes loans and provides backing for projects which will benefit the European Communities. Its head office is in Luxembourg, and all member states of the Communities have shares in it. European Investment Bank (EIB).
Banque française du commerce extérieur—a bank which specialises in handling foreign trade with France.
Banque de l'Indochine—one of the major French private banks, with extensive holdings abroad.
Banque de Paris et des Pays-bas (Paribas)—a private deposit bank, part of the *Compagnie financière de Paris et des Pays-bas*, one of the largest private banking organisations.
Banque des règlements internationaux (BRI)—Bank for International Settlements (BIS).
Caisse des dépôts et consignations—provides loans for local authority housing projects and holds the deposits of the *caisses d'épargne*.
Caisse nationale des marchés de l'Etat (CNME)—provides loans for public bodies and nationalised industry.
Compagnie financière de Suez et de l'union parisienne—a large private banking group.
compte courant postal/compte chèque postal (CCP)—a current account facility provided by the French Post Office.
Conseil national du crédit—a body which, in conjunction with the *Banque de France*, regulates the supply of credit within the country.
Cour des comptes—a legal and administrative institution which pronounces upon financial matters regarding the State and all bodies receiving public money. Audit court.
Crédit agricole—a state-controlled credit establishment specialising in loans for agricultural purposes.
Crédit foncier—a state-controlled credit establishment which provides loans for house-building.

Crédit national—a body which grants long- and medium-term loans for the development of industry.

Fonds monétaire international (FMI)—International Monetary Fund (IMF).

société immobilière pour le commerce et l'industrie (SICOMI)—a type of company which provides finance for the leasing and purchase of business premises, using the form of financing known as *crédit-bail*.

société d'investissements à capital variable (SICAV)—unit trust company.

trésor public—a branch of the *Ministère de l'économie* which acts as "public purse" in holding and distributing public funds on both a national and local level. It also plays a part in the administration of the country's banking system and money market. It is not the equivalent of the British Treasury, which has much wider powers.

zone franc—the area of the world in which the French franc is used as the basic unit for monetary conversion, viz. France, the *Départements d'outre-mer*, the *Territoires d'outre-mer*, and some other states which used to be under French rule. It is not equivalent to the sterling area, because in the *zone franc* the French franc is not necessarily legal tender, as the pound sterling is in the sterling area.

VI THE LEGAL SYSTEM

The French legal system differs so fundamentally from the British one that it would be futile to attempt a comparison between the two. Their offices and institutions, while they might in some cases bear a superficial resemblance to each other, are typically based on very different concepts and thus fulfil different functions.

The Law

The British system is founded on a tradition of common law, applicable to all, and interpreted by individual judges when a statute is not clear so as to provide a precedent for future reference. In France, however, private law *(le droit privé)* consists, in the main, of a number of *Codes,* each containing legislation relating to a single area (e.g. *Code de commerce, Code pénal, Code du travail*), which provide a definitive statement of the law as it stands.

Administrative law is not codified and, like British legislation, consists of a mass of sometimes conflicting statutes made unsystematically as the need arose. Consequently, the judges in administrative courts need to be specialists in this field, the principles of which are in many ways quite different from those of private law.

Laws *(lois)* can only be introduced, repealed or amended by the legislative procedure described in Chapter I, although *règlements* relating to minor matters can be made by the administration.

Perhaps the most marked difference between the British and French systems lies in the latter's institution of *séparation des pouvoirs,* which creates a formal and absolute distinction between the judiciary on the one hand and the legislative and executive authorities on the other. Thus, members of the judiciary can play no part in the making of new laws and regulations, nor do they have any power to judge members of the administration or legislature, their jurisdiction being confined to the areas of civil and criminal law which make up *l'ordre de juridiction judiciaire.*

Cases involving the administration are dealt with by the administrative courts which constitute *l'ordre de juridiction administrative.* If any uncertainty should arise as to which court is competent to judge a particular case, the *tribunal des conflits* decides which court is appropriate.

Civil and criminal courts

The lowest level of jurisdiction in the non-administrative courts is represented mainly by the *tribunal d'instance civil,* which deals with civil cases involving small sums of money, and the *tribunal de police,* which deals with offences constituting a *contravention* (a petty offence punishable by a fine). There is generally one of each type of *tribunal* in every *arrondissement* and, in addition, some major cities also have their own *tribunal de police,* which deals with *contraventions.* All these courts are presided over by a single judge.

There are also a number of specialised courts at this level such as the *tribunaux pour mineurs* (juvenile courts), *conseils des prud'hommes* (industrial arbitration courts), *tribunaux paritaires de baux ruraux* (which judge on matters relating to agricultural tenancies), *tribunaux de commerce* (commercial courts), *commissions de première instance de sécurité sociale* (courts dealing with disputes arising from the *sécurité sociale* system), and the *tribunal permanent des forces armées* (military court). The composition of these specialised courts (called *tribunaux d'exception*) varies according to their individual needs.

More serious cases are dealt with by courts of a higher level. Civil cases involving large sums are judged in the *tribunal de grande instance civil,* while criminal cases in which the offence constitutes a *délit* (crime of a fairly serious nature) are judged by the *tribunal correctionnel* (equivalent to a *tribunal de grande instance criminel*). Each of these courts consists of three *juges* (judges), aided by a *procureur de la République,* who represents the *ministère public,* and a *greffier* (see below). Courts of this level are found in the *chef-lieu* of every *département,* and there may be additional ones in other major towns. They sit whenever they are needed.

All the courts mentioned so far are classed as *tribunaux de première instance.* Above them are the higher courts, known as *cours,* of which there are three types dealing with non-administrative cases. The first is the *cour d'assises,* which sits only at certain times of the year to try people accused of *crimes* (major crimes). These courts, of which there is one in every *département,* each consist of three judges and a *jury* of nine people chosen at random from a list of those eligible.

The second court at this level is the *cour d'appel* (appeals court), of which there are 28 in mainland France, each serving several *départements.* The court is usually divided into two or more *chambres* which specialise in different types of case (e.g. *chambre commerciale, chambre des appels correctionnels,* etc.). There are generally five *magistrats* (judges) in a *cour d'appel* and their final decision is called an *arrêt.* Most cases from all the *tribunaux* have the right of appeal.

The third court of this level is the *Cour de cassation,* which sits in Paris. It is divided into 5 *chambres civiles* and 1 *chambre criminelle,* and is composed of the most senior judges. Its function is not to judge a case on its merits, but to decide whether or not the judgement of a lower court was correctly given from a purely legal point of view. Cases from the *cours d'appel* and the *cours d'assises* may be brought before the *Cour de cassation,* as well as those cases from the other *tribunaux* which were not open to appeal.

The *Président de la République* has the right to reprieve a convicted person *(droit de grâce).*

Judicial Personnel

At the head of the judicial hierarchy of private law is the *Ministre de la justice*, known as the *Garde des sceaux*, but his responsibilities are at the level of the Government rather than the courts. The process of judging cases is carried out by *magistrats* of the *corps judiciaire* who, unlike British judges, were not originally lawyers, but instead are trained in law specifically for the purpose of becoming *magistrats*, and have a career structure similar to that of civil servants. They also differ from the British judiciary in that they are attached to a particular court, not a circuit, and in that all *magistrats* are full-time professional judges. (In the *tribunaux d'exception*, however, cases are judged by specialists in the field concerned who are not *magistrats*.)

There are two types of *magistrat*, known collectively as the *magistrature assise* or *siège*, and the *magistrature debout* or *parquet*. It is the *magistrats du siège* who do the actual judging of both civil and criminal cases. Although they are *fonctionnaires*, they are independent of any authorities and enjoy, amongst other privileges, that of *inamovibilité*, which means that they cannot be transferred or dismissed except in cases of grave professional misconduct.

The *magistrats du parquet*, on the other hand, are *amovibles*, which means that they may be dismissed or suspended. The *parquet* is also known as the *ministère public* and plays a very important role in legal proceedings. In general, the *ministère public* represents the law, and members of it are present at the *cour de cassation*, the *cours d'appel* and the *tribunaux de grande instance*. In civil courts its members are responsible for the presentation and explanation of the law in an objective, theoretical manner, and for recommending to the court, in the form of *conclusions*, a line of action which may help the *magistrats du siège* to make a correct judgement. The role of the *ministère public* in criminal cases is that of public prosecutor.

A number of other people are qualified to perform legal tasks both inside and outside the courts. They are known collectively as *auxiliaires de justice* and belong to several different professions.

It is the *avocat* who puts his client's case verbally before the court and who prepares all the necessary documents beforehand. In a *cour d'appel*, however, this latter duty is performed by an *avoué*, although a reform of the legal profession in 1972 abolished the title of *avoué* in all the other courts. In theory the function of an *avoué* is held to be that of representing his client, while the function of the *avocat* is to give the client assistance in court, but in practice the distinction between the two had become somewhat blurred, hence the reform of the profession.

Both *avocats* and *avoués* must have the qualifications of a *maîtrise en droit* and a *certificat d'aptitude à la profession d'avocat*, as well as some professional training. Before they can practise they must also register with the *barreau* (or in the case of *avoués*, the *cour d'appel*) in their area, although they are free to practise elsewhere. For administrative purposes each *barreau* elects a *conseil*, which is presided over by a *bâtonnier*. There is no limit on the number of practising *avocats* (whose income derives from the fees paid by their clients), but the number of *avoués* is restricted by law.

Outside the courtroom an extremely important figure is the *notaire* who, besides advising his clients on legal matters, also has the power to authenticate and witness legal documents. In French law, *actes sous seing privé* (privately signed documents) must, should a dispute arise, be proved authentic, whereas *actes authentiques* (documents signed in the presence of a *notaire*) are held to be valid unless they can be proved false. The latter proof can only be made by means of an *inscription de faux,* a very seldom-used procedure. *Notaires* are paid by their clients, but the law sets a limit on the number who can practise at any one time.

Another official whose main work is done outside the courts is the *huissier de justice* (bailiff), who is responsible for serving summonses and other documents, and for ensuring that various instructions given by the court are carried out. The *huissier* also has some administrative duties inside the courtroom, in which circumstances his British equivalent would be the court usher.

Secretarial duties such as minute-taking, transcription and registration inside the courts are performed by a service department known as the *secrétariat-greffe,* which consists of a number of *secrétaires-greffiers.*

Judicial procedure
1. *Civil cases*

A *procès civil* (civil case) must go through several stages before the judges (or judge) come to their final decision. The first preliminary step is the *citation,* in which the *demandeur* (plaintiff, claimant) informs the *défendeur* (defendant) of his intention to prosecute him. The *exploit d'ajournement* (summons) is delivered by a *huissier* and contains the name of the plaintiff's *avocat* and details of the time and place at which the next stage of the case will be heard.

If he wishes to be present at the hearing in order to defend himself the defendant may also employ an *avocat,* who will appear before the *tribunal* on his client's behalf. This appearance is known as *comparution.* Then follows the *mise au rôle* when, on the presentation by the plaintiff's lawyer of a document called a *"placet",* which sets out the plaintiff's claim, the case will be registered at the *greffe.*

After these preliminaries comes the first stage of the hearing proper, the *audience de liaison d'instance,* the date of which is stated in a document called an *avenir,* sent to the defendant's lawyer by that of the plaintiff. It is at this stage that the case begins to follow a procedure totally different from that of English law. The lawyers must each submit to the court their *conclusions,* which are documents containing a detailed account of the arguments which will be put forward on behalf of their respective clients. They must also make a declaration of all other items they will use in evidence.

This is followed by the *instruction* and *administration des preuves,* supervised in the *tribunaux de grande instance* and the *cours d'appel* by the *magistrat de la mise en état,* and in other courts by the *magistrat chargé de suivre la procédure.* In this procedure the lawyers on both sides are required to deposit all the documents and other items of evidence with the court, so that both they and the judge can familiarise themselves with all the relevant information. When this is finished the judge officially terminates the proceedings with an *ordonnance de clôture.*

The case then goes into its next stage, the *audience* (hearing), which takes place in court and is usually open to the public. Here the lawyers of both parties must argue their respective cases verbally, in a speech called a *plaidoirie.* This is followed by the *conclusions* of the *ministère public,* which constitute a statement of the legal aspects of the case. When this is finished the judges retire for the *délibéré,* during which time they make their decision. (There is never a jury in a civil case.) The *jugement* (judgement) may be given either straight after the *délibéré* or, if the judges need more time to consider, after an interval of a week or two. As soon as it has been given verbally, a written copy of the *jugement* is sent to both parties by the *huissier.* This is normally the end of a civil case.

If, however, one of the parties is dissatisfied with the outcome of the case, he may demand that it be heard by the *cour d'appel.* In order to do this the procedure followed is very similar to that of the lower courts, except that it is an *avoué à la cour d'appel* who is responsible for the preparation of the documents to be used in the case. The *plaidoirie,* however, is still given by the *avocat.* The final decision of the *cour d'appel* is called an *arrêt.*

If one of the parties is still not satisfied and thinks the court's decision was ill-founded, the case may go before one of the *chambres civiles* of the *Cour de cassation* in Paris. To do this a specially qualified lawyer, known as an *avocat au Conseil d'Etat et à la Cour de cassation,* must present to the court a *pourvoi en cassation,* which is a request for the decision to be quashed. If the judges consider that the decision of the court in question was made in error, it will be quashed *(cassé)* and the case sent back to another court of the same level to be retried. If the judgement of the second court is questioned the case may be heard by a plenary session of the *Cour de cassation* and the resulting decision will be final.

2. Criminal cases

The first stage of a criminal case is the *mise en accusation* which is usually made by the *procureur de la République* (public prosecutor), although other authorities and private citizens also have the right to do this. (The victim of a crime may at the same time take out an *action civile* suit against the accused for compensation.)

This is followed by the *enquête préliminaire,* during which the police must satisfy the *procureur de la République* that evidence exists for a case to be brought against the accused. In some cases, such as where the accused is caught *en flagrant délit* (in the act of committing a crime), this is merely a formality, whereas in others it needs more time. If the evidence seems conclusive the accused receives a *citation directe,* which is a summons to appear before a court. If, however, further evidence is deemed necessary the *procureur de la République* requests, by means of a document called a *réquisitoire,* that additional evidence be collected. This procedure is the *instruction* and is supervised by a *juge d'instruction* (a *magistrat du siège* attached to a *tribunal de grande instance*), who is responsible for obtaining statements and material evidence, and for carrying out the formalities necessary for prosecution.

If at the end of the *instruction* the evidence is found to be insufficient, a declaration of *non-lieu* is made and the case is dropped. If, on the other hand, adequate evidence has been amassed, the case goes on to the final stage, which is the hearing in court. During this, verbal arguments are made by the lawyers of both parties and, after the written and verbal evidence has been examined, a decision is made either by the judges or, in more serious cases, by a *jury* of nine people. If the accused is found guilty *(coupable)* he is then sentenced by the *président* of the court, who is one of the judges.

A convicted person may, if he is not satisfied with the court's decision, take his case either to a *cour d'appel* or to the *Cour de cassation.*

Administrative courts

Cases tried by the administrative courts fall into two categories; those which involve the administration as a body (e.g. where a *règlement* is thought to be illegal and unfair), and those in which an individual *fonctionnaire* is alleged to have broken the law in the course of his duties. (There are a few exceptions to the latter part of this rule, such as motoring offences, which are always tried by the civil courts.)

The *droit administratif* relating to the administration in France is, in many ways, different from the *droit privé* and the *droit public* which apply to non-administrative areas. In the field of contract, for instance, the administration may impose conditions unilaterally, a right which other contractors do not enjoy. If, however, the administration exceeds its powers in any way, then members of the public, either as individuals or as organisations, may institute proceedings against it in the administrative courts.

Most cases brought against the administration are heard by one of the *tribunaux administratifs* of which there are 25 in France. Each *tribunal* consists of a *président* and four *conseillers,* of whom the overwhelming majority are recruited from graduates of the ENA. The *corps* that they form belongs to the administrative structure of the *Ministère de l'intérieur,* unlike that of the judiciary, which is administered by the *Ministère de la justice.*

If either party is not satisfied with the judgement delivered in a *tribunal administratif* then the case may be brought before the *Conseil d'Etat,* which functions as a *cour d'appel* and a *cour de cassation* in administrative cases. Some serious legislative matters, such as questioning the legality of a new *règlement,* are brought before the *Conseil d'Etat* without going through any lesser courts because it is the only body competent to deal with such cases.

Within the system of public law there are also a number of specialised courts dealing with particular types of case. Some of these are in Paris (e.g. *Cour des comptes, Cour de discipline budgétaire*), while others, which are not courts as such, but have the status of *juridictions administratives d'attribution*, are found at the level of the *département* or *région* (e.g. *commissions d'aide sociale*). There are also bodies with the status of courts, the purpose of which is to ensure that standards of ethics are maintained inside the various professions found within the administration (e.g. *Conseil supérieur de l'éducation nationale*). Cases from any of these specialised courts may ultimately be taken before the *Conseil d'Etat*.

The procedure followed in administrative courts is different in many ways from that followed in the civil courts. It is further complicated by the fact that it also varies from one type of *tribunal* to another, so that it is not possible to give a general picture.

GLOSSARY

abrogation—the nullification of one law by another later one. Repeal, rescission.
accise—a type of indirect tax. Excise.
accord—agreement, treaty.
accusation: mise en a.—arraignment (see text).
acquis—patrimony.
acquit—acquittal.
acte authentique—authenticated document (see text).
acte sous seing privé—privately signed document (see text).
acte sur papier timbré—official document.
action (en justice)—legal action, lawsuit.
action civile—civil case.
aide judiciaire—legal aid.
amende—fine.
amiable compositeur—an informal arbitrator between two disputing parties, who have agreed to accept his decision.
appel—appeal (see text).
auditeur de justice—see *Ecole nationale de la magistrature*.
avenir—writ of summons (see text).
avocat—lawyer (see text).
avoué—lawyer (see text).
ayant cause/ayant droit—a person who derives a right from another person (see Chapter VII).
bail—a type of lease.
barreau—Bar association (see text).
blâme—a disciplinary measure which can be taken against lawyers by their professional association. Reprimand.
bordereau—a document enabling a creditor to obtain what is owed to him. Schedule.
cession-bail—lease-back, i.e. the sale of property to an institution which leases it to the vendor for a period of years.
circonstances atténuantes—extenuating circumstances.
collège des magistrats—a group of *magistrats* of a *cour d'appel* who are elected by their peers to perform various internal administrative duties.

collégialité—the system whereby a number (always uneven) of judges sit in the same court.

comparaître—to appear before a court.

conseil juridique—an authorised consulting lawyer, i.e. a lawyer with specific qualifications entitling him to offer his services for consultation.

conseil des prud'hommes—industrial arbitration court (see text).

Conseil supérieur de la magistrature—a body presided over by the *Président de la République,* responsible for the nomination and disciplining of judges, as they are not answerable to any other authority.

conseiller juridique—legal adviser, in a general sense.

contentieux—a group of legal cases belonging to the same category, e.g. *le contentieux pénal.*

coupable—guilty party.

Cour de sûreté de l'Etat—a court responsible for judging cases involving State security.

crédit-bail—leasing.

crédit-croisé—swap.

culpabilité—guilt.

curateur—a person who, in legal matters, assists an adult who is physically or mentally handicapped. Trustee, guardian.

délibéré—judges' consultation (see text).

demande en justice—petition, bill of complaint.

demande reconventionnelle—countersuit.

demandeur—plaintiff, petitioner, claimant (see text).

dépens—costs (paid by the loser of a case to the winner to cover the latter's legal expenses).

descente sur les lieux—a visit by the judge and other officials to the scene of a crime.

dessaisissement du juge—at the end of a case, when he has delivered judgement, the judge is *dessaisi,* that is he should normally have nothing more to do with the case.

dol—in a contract, deliberate misrepresentation by one party in order to gain some advantage from the other. Fraudulent misrepresentation.

domicile—principal residential address (see *résidence*).

dommages-intérêts—damages.

droit administratif—administrative law (see text).

droit commun—the laws which are generally applicable in a given field, usually that of civil law; ordinary law. The courts known as *juridictions de droit commun* are, in the civil courts the *tribunaux de grande instance* and the *cours d'appel,* in the criminal courts the *tribunaux correctionnels* and *cours d'appel,* and in the administrative courts the *tribunaux administratifs.* They have this title because they are empowered to judge all types of case within that field, apart from those which come under the jurisdiction of the *tribunaux d'exception.*

droit coutumier—common law.

Ecole nationale de la magistrature (ENM)—a post-university educational establishment responsible for training judges. The students first become *auditeurs de justice,* then on graduating may become *magistrats.*

écrou—the registration of a prisoner in a prison.

éducation surveillée—a general name given to the special schools and other arrangements provided for the supervision of young offenders.

emphytéose—a type of long-term lease (can be up to 99 years).

emprise—the act by which the administrative authorities take possession, legally or otherwise, of property belonging to a private citizen. He may in some cases be eligible for compensation. Emprise.

entrer en vigueur—come into force.

équité—"natural justice", equity.

ester en justice—to take part, in some capacity, in a legal case; to go to law.

exhérédation—disinheritance.

expédition—an authenticated copy of an original document, which can only be obtained from the official who holds the original.

exploit d'ajournement—summons to appear (see text).

flagrant délit: en f.d.—in the act of committing a crime.

fongible—mutually replaceable, fungible.

force majeure—circumstances which could not possibly have been foreseen.

forfaiture—a crime committed by a civil servant in the course of his duties.

grâce—reprieve (see text).

greffe—see *secrétariat-greffe*.

greffier—see *secrétaire-greffier*.

grief: acte faisant g.—an administrative course of action liable to give grounds for complaint.

Haute cour de justice—a court which meets only when circumstances demand in order to try a *Président de la République,* members of the Government or their accomplices accused of high treason.

heures légales—the time between 6 a.m. and 9 p.m. outside which legal formalities cannot be executed.

à huis clos—"in camera".

imprévision—a theory according to which a person or company under contract to the administration can ask for the contract to be altered if unforeseen events seriously affect the agreed charges or prices.

inamovibilité—tenure (see text).

inculpation—a document in which the *juge d'instruction* states that he wishes further evidence to be gathered against a suspected offender. Indictment, charge.

inculpé—accused.

infraction—offence. There are three types of *infraction*: *contravention, délit* and *crime* (see text).

instance—a series of procedural formalities constituting a trial. Lawsuit.

internement administratif—internment.

juge de l'application des peines—a judge in a *tribunal de grande instance* responsible for supervising the execution of the punishment.

juge-commissaire—a judge designated to supervise the carrying out of some given legal procedure.

juge consulaire—a judge in a *tribunal de commerce*.

juge des enfants—a judge in a juvenile court.

juge de l'exécution—a single judge in a *tribunal de grande instance* who supervises the execution of judgements.

juge de l'expropriation—a judge in a *tribunal de grande instance* who fixes the amount of compensation to be paid to someone who has been expropriated.

juge. de loyers—a judge responsible for settling differences relating to lettings of various types.

juge rapporteur—this role is fulfilled by the *juge de la mise en état* when he presents his report *(rapport)* to the court, before the *plaidoiries*.

juge unique—a judge who carries out his duties alone, rather than forming part of a panel *(formation collégiale)*. A single judge is found mainly in the lower courts.

juridiction—a group of courts of the same type and level.

juridictions de droit commun—see *droit commun.*
juridictions d'exception—specialised courts (see text).
jurisconsulte—a person engaged in the academic study of law and who may be consulted on points of law which arise. Jurist, legal expert.
légitime défense—self-defence.
liberté surveillée—probation.
litiges—litigation, lawsuit.
loi—statute, law, Act of Parliament (see text and Chapter I).
magistrat—judge (see text).
maison d'arrêt, de correction—short-term prison.
maison centrale—long-term prison.
mandat d'arrêt—arrest warrant.
motif—ground.
moyen—ground.
nomenclature juridique—the system of references used to identify sources of legal information and texts.
notaire—notary (see text).
officier public—an official with the authority to authenticate various legal documents.
ordre des avocats—a term referring to all the *avocats* attached to one *barreau.* Bar.
pécule—sum of money given to a prisoner on his leaving prison, earned by him by virtue of work done while detained.
peine—punishment.
personne civile/juridique—a person who has rights, duties, etc. within the law. This applies to all human beings. Legal person.
personne morale—a corporate body endowed with a personality for the purposes of the law, e.g. a *société anonyme.* A *personne morale* is also a *personne juridique.*
personne physique—natural person.
plaider—plead.
plaidoirie—counsel's speech (see text).
plainte—complaint, indictment.
poursuivre en justice—prosecute, take legal action against.
préemption—a right to purchase property or goods put up for sale publicly in preference to other prospective buyers. Pre-emption.
préjudice—injury, damage, loss, detriment.
preuves—evidence, proof.
procès—trial, court case, proceedings.
procès-verbal—record of statements, official report.
procureur général—a *magistrat* in charge of the *ministère public* at the *Cour de cassation* or a *cour d'appel.*
radiation—disbarring, striking off. The ultimate punishment for an *avocat.*
récépissé—receipt for something deposited.
reçu—receipt.
récuser—to demand that a judge or other official stand down because of alleged partiality.
registre du rôle—a register of the cases to be heard before the court (see text).
résidence—address where a person is living, as opposed to his *domicile,* or legal address.
saisie—attachment, distraint.
saisine—seisin.
saisir la justice—to take action in court.

secrétaire-greffier—clerk of the court (see text).
secrétariat-greffe—registry (see text).
statut—article of association, rule, regulation.
tierce opposition—a means by which a person adversely affected by the outcome of a case, but not one of the parties involved, can appeal against the decision.
tribunal—court, bench, tribunal (see text).
tutelle—guardianship.

VII SOCIAL SERVICES

1. Insurance schemes

a) La Sécurité sociale

In France, as in Britain, virtually the whole of the population is insured against economic hardship caused by factors beyond the control of the individual. The French system of social insurance *(la Sécurité sociale)* does, however, differ radically from the British National Insurance scheme both in its practical organisation and in the philosophy upon which it is founded.

One of the most notable features of the French system is that it consists of not one but several schemes covering various sections of the working population, each scheme having its own rates of contribution (paid partially by the employee, partially by the employer) and of benefit. This situation arose because in 1945, when the present system was instituted, certain groups of workers already had their own schemes which offered more favourable terms than did the new system, so they insisted on remaining outside the main scheme. As a result there now exist *régimes spéciaux* (special schemes) for miners, seamen, agricultural workers, railwaymen, civil servants, workers in some nationalised industries and for various categories of the self-employed, as well as the *régime général* (general scheme), which covers other employees.

The bodies responsible for the day-to-day running of the *Sécurité sociale* do not form part of any State-owned system (although naturally they are subject to a good deal of legislative constraint), but instead are designated private organisations providing a public service. In each *département* there are two types of office dealing with claims and benefits; first, the *caisses primaires d'assurance maladie,* responsible for the administration of medical insurance, maternity insurance, death benefits and insurance against industrial disease and injury; secondly, the *caisses d'allocations familiales,* which deal with family allowances and related benefits. There is also a *union de recouvrement* in each *département,* which looks after the money paid as contributions into the *caisses,* each of which is financially independent.

Each office *(caisse)* is administered by a *conseil d'administration,* consisting of representatives of the larger trade unions, the self-employed and employers, in equal numbers, all of whom hold office for four years. Members of the different branches of the medical profession are also represented in an advisory capacity.

Continuing up the hierarchy, there is a *caisse régionale d'assurance maladie* for every *région,* which decides and administers the rates of payment of industrial injury benefits and carries out programmes to encourage health and safety at work, as well as providing various social services. It is also responsible, at present, for some of the formalities connected with old-age pensions (except for the *caisses régionales* in Paris and Strasbourg, where there are different arrangements).

On the national level, there are three bodies responsible for the administration of the three sections of the *Sécurité sociale*; the *Caisse nationale d'assurance maladie*, the *Caisse nationale d'allocations familiales*, and the *Caisse nationale d'assurance vieillesse*, which together form the *Union des caisses nationales de sécurité sociale (UCANSS)*. The finances of these three offices are administered by the *Agence centrale des organismes de sécurité sociale*, which receives the contributions collected by the *unions de recouvrement* in the *départements*.

Several ministerial departments are also concerned with the administration of the *Sécurité sociale*. Legal texts and directives relating to it are prepared in a department of the *Ministère de la santé et de la famille*; its accounts are audited by the *Cour des comptes*; its dealings with the *trésor public* are carried out by the *Ministère de l'économie*. There is also an *Inspection générale de la sécurité sociale*, which supervises and coordinates the operations of the numerous bodies connected with the *Sécurité sociale*, and acts as a link between them and government departments.

The administration of the *régimes spéciaux* varies with each scheme, but is broadly similar to that of the *régime général*. Some schemes in fact operate within the administrative structure of the *régime général*, while others have their own offices and organisation.

The benefits to which insured persons and their dependents are entitled under the *régime général* of the *Sécurité sociale* can be divided broadly into three areas; medical benefits, family allowances and old-age pensions.

There is no free medical service in France as there is in Britain. Instead, the patient pays directly for the services of a doctor of his choice and is then reimbursed by the *Sécurité sociale* for between 70% and 100% of the cost, depending on the type of treatment involved. The difference between the cost and the amount reimbursed is known as the *participation de l'assuré aux tarifs servant de base au calcul des prestations*, more commonly referred to as the *"ticket modérateur"*, and is intended to discourage patients from seeking unnecessary treatment. The fees charged by doctors within the *Sécurité sociale* system are the result of an agreement *(convention)* between representatives of the medical profession and the *caisse nationale d'assurance maladie*, and it is a percentage of these fees which is reimbursed. Although most doctors participate in the insurance scheme, there are still a few who do not, and they are free to charge whatever fees they please, so that the patient who consults a doctor "privately" will have to bear the difference in cost himself and is also reimbursed for a smaller percentage of the standard fee. The same is true of hospital treatment, which can take place in a public *hôpital* or a private *clinique*. This dual system does lead to some imbalance in and duplication of medical facilities, as there is a tendency for private clinics (which provide a third of all hospital beds in France) to specialise in fields which have a high profit and a low capital outlay (e.g. maternity, minor surgery), leaving the more costly forms of treatment to the public sector, which is forced to charge higher fees as a consequence.

In the event of injuries sustained at work or occupational illnesses, the patient does not have to pay for his treatment, the cost of which is borne directly by the *caisse primaire,* unless he chooses to be treated in a private clinic, in which case he must pay the difference in cost himself. While he is unable to work, the victim of such an accident or disease also receives a certain amount of injury benefit.

As a result of France's post-war policy encouraging a higher birthrate, maternity benefits and family allowances are particularly high compared with those in Britain. Expectant mothers who are eligible for *Sécurité sociale* benefits, either in their own right or because they are dependent on an insured husband or father, are entitled to payments from the *assurance maternité* section of medical insurance, through which they are reimbursed for all medical expenses connected with the pregnancy. Women who are insured in their own right also receive an allowance amounting to 90% of their salary for the six weeks preceding and eight weeks following the birth. All pregnant women receive *allocations prénatales* (pre-natal allowances) on condition that they are examined by a doctor at certain prescribed intervals, in accordance with the regulations concerning *la protection maternelle et infantile (PMI)* (maternal and infant protection). After the birth itself, if the child is born alive, they also receive *allocations postnatales* (post-natal allowances), which are paid at intervals for each child during its first 2 years, on condition that it is examined regularly by a doctor.

Quite substantial *allocations familiales* (family allowances) are paid to families with children, especially if there are three or more, in which case it is designated a *famille nombreuse.* (There are also other benefits available for *familles nombreuses,* such as reduced rail fares, but these are not part of the *Sécurité sociale.*) If only one parent is working, the family may be entitled to an *allocation de salaire unique* (single-wage allowance), or if the father is self-employed, to an *allocation de la mère au foyer* (mother-at-home allowance), both of which benefits are means-tested. Single parents may also be entitled to an *allocation pour frais de garde* (childminding allowance). These last three allowances have now been replaced by the *complément familial* (family supplement), which will benefit a greater number of families. Some families, if they fulfil certain criteria relating to income, family size and rent, may also receive an *allocation de logement* (housing allowance), which is calculated as a percentage of the difference between the real rent and a hypothetical minimum rent.

The third main area of benefits within the *Sécurité sociale* is the *assurance vieillesse* (old-age insurance), which is extremely complex, owing to the number of changes in pension schemes which have taken place during the lifetimes of present-day beneficiaries. Under the *régime général,* on retirement at 60, an employee who has contributed for between 15 and 30 years receives a pension amounting to 25% of a theoretical basic salary calculated on the basis of the best 10 years of his past earnings and on present-day wage rates. If he remains at work and does not claim his pension (which he can do even if he continues working), the pension is increased by 3.75% of the basic salary for every year after the age of 60, up to a maximum total of 50%.

The *régimes spéciaux* differ from the *régime général* in that the pension is usually awarded earlier (in some cases at 55 or even 50) and the benefits are substantially higher. Unlike those in the *régime général*, these pensions cannot be claimed before retirement from the occupation to which the scheme is attached, but the retired pensioner is free to find another job if he wishes without it affecting his pension. The *régimes spéciaux* also pay out extra benefits for pensioners who have had children, but do not allow more for dependent wives.

There are still some old people who retired before they had had time to make sufficient contributions to the *Sécurité sociale* to qualify for a pension. Nevertheless, if they can provide proof of having been employed for twenty-five years, they are eligible for the *allocation aux vieux travailleurs salariés (AVTS)*, which is a means-tested benefit. Although it cannot strictly speaking be termed insurance, the AVTS is also paid out of the funds of the *Sécurité sociale*.

The pensions paid under the schemes for the self-employed are calculated using different systems from that of the *régime général*, most of which involve the accumulation of *points de retraite* (pension points), the value of which is related to current incomes and cost of living. Although the schemes are quite flexible, the benefits paid out are generally lower than under the *régime général*. In these schemes, too, there is a means-tested element which is payable if the pensioner has not made enough contributions to qualify for an adequate pension.

b) Les régimes complémentaires

As well as contributing to one of the basic schemes of the *Sécurité sociale*, workers and employers in many sectors of French industry and commerce are also required by law to contribute towards one of the *régimes complémentaires* (complementary schemes), which exist because of a demand among higher-paid workers to supplement the extremely low benefits paid out by the basic schemes. These complementary schemes were originally the result of agreements between individual employers or groups of employers and their employees, but French law allows an agreement between two parties to be generalised to cover other parties in a similar situation, so contribution to these schemes is now obligatory for a large number of workers.

Although the complementary schemes are outside the general scheme, they are not equivalent to British private or occupational pension schemes, which are voluntary. They are financially independent, but subject to a good deal of State supervision, and must have half their reserves invested in State securities. Nor do they operate on a funded basis, as is the case with the British private schemes, but instead, like the *régime général*, use a system called *répartition*, which means that the contributions collected now are used to pay the pensions of people who may not have contributed fully or even at all to the scheme. The philosophy behind this is the principle of solidarity between generations, rather than that of receiving only what one has paid for.

The benefits paid by the complementary schemes are mainly in the form of old-age pensions of one type or another, along with widows' pensions, some child benefits and some help with medical fees. There are now also complementary schemes providing unemployment insurance, for which no statutory provision exists within the *Sécurité sociale*.

c) Les mutuelles

In addition to the compulsory insurance schemes there are also a number of *mutuelles* (friendly societies) which are voluntary schemes, open to people who fulfil some kind of condition, usually of employment or residence. They generally provide assistance with medical expenses and some other types of welfare provision such as holiday camps for children.

2. Non-contributory benefits

Most French people are insured by the *Sécurité sociale* either in their own right or by virtue of their being dependent on a contributor *(les ayants droit)*. Nevertheless, there are still some people who are not insured, or who find themselves in a position of not fulfilling the necessary conditions which would entitle them to benefit. For these people there exist a number of sources of help to which they may apply.

a) L'Aide sociale

The most important of these sources is *l'Aide sociale* (social aid), which although it provides assistance to the very needy, cannot really be equated with the British Supplementary Benefits scheme. Most of the administration for *l'Aide sociale* is done at the level of the *commune*, as all but the smallest *communes* have a local office to which potential beneficiaries must apply. For both statutory and discretionary benefits the applicant must undergo a rigorous means-test, which is carried out by local officials, and if there is a possibility that he is eligible for benefit the claim is then passed on to the *commission d'admission* of the *département*. This procedure can take several weeks, during which time the applicant must fend for himself, although there is some provision for emergency payments.

Each local office is financially autonomous, but the largest proportion of its revenue comes from the central government. The amount allocated to each *département* for statutory assistance varies according to its needs and resources. In addition, each *commune* has a second budget which it uses to finance discretionary payments of social aid, although before money can be allocated for discretionary aid all the statutory payments must have been made.

The statutory benefits paid by *l'Aide sociale* cover eleven categories of need which are strictly defined by the regulations. Several of these can be classed as medical aid, which includes payment of the *"ticket modérateur"*, payment of insurance contributions on behalf of those who are not themselves in a position to do so, free treatment for sufferers from long illnesses such as tuberculosis and mental illness, and allowances for the blind or severely handicapped. When assistance is given with medical fees the patient is much more restricted than usual in his choice of doctor.

A large part of the *Aide sociale* budget is spent on aid to children, either in institutions of various types or within their families. Payments are frequently made when there is a danger that parents might abandon their children, and also if the family does not qualify for the *allocations familiales,* although the latter case is extremely rare these days. Parents of handicapped children may also receive some allowances. If a family's breadwinner is doing compulsory military service they are also eligible for assistance from the State, although nowadays men with dependent families are not conscripted.

There are also numerous benefits available for old people, some of whom have an extremely low income, although they are more likely to receive help in kind than in cash, especially outside the major urban centres. They can be visited by a home help from *l'aide ménagère* (home help service), who is paid by the *commune,* and can receive small amounts of food, clothing and fuel. Many *communes* provide restaurant, laundry and other facilities for old people as a group, a practice which the government is now encouraging. Another benefit for which some old people are eligible is the *allocation de loyer* (rent allowance), which pays a certain proportion of their rent. If they are unable to look after themselves on their own, old people may be given places in residential homes, or their families may receive an allowance so that they can live in the family's home. In some cases where their income is very low, old or disabled people may qualify for an *allocation supplémentaire du Fonds national de solidarité,* a fund specially set up for this purpose.

Many old people, however, do not claim the benefits to which they might be entitled, partly because the application procedure is extremely complicated, and partly because of the extensive means-testing to which they would be subject. Not only are the applicant's own means investigated in great detail (including such resources as a vegetable garden, livestock and gifts from charities), but also those of his children, grandchildren and other close relatives, who are deemed to have a legal duty to support the elderly in the family *(obligation alimentaire).* Even if assistance is granted to the applicant, the *commune* is empowered to claim the money back from the estate when the recipient dies *(recouvrement sur succession),* a practice which, although infrequently used, is sufficient to deter many old people from claiming assistance.

Apart from children's and old people's homes, the *commune* may also make some provision in short-stay hostels for some categories of homeless. The residents must fulfil certain conditions, and are required to register for work or undergo rehabilitation training. Some *communes* also provide *ateliers protégés* (sheltered workshops) for people unable to cope with a normal work environment.

b)   Other services provided by the local authorities

In addition to assistance given to individuals, local authorities all over France are now being encouraged to provide facilities which will benefit whole sections of the community, regardless of their economic circumstances. There are numerous provisions for young people, such as subsidised hostels for young workers *(foyers de jeunes travailleurs)*, and canteens for schoolchildren, students and other young people. Most larger *communes* have a *maison des jeunes et de la culture*, a type of youth and community centre where sports, films, handicrafts and many other cultural activities take place. Old people are catered for with day centres, canteens and other facilities. People of all ages benefit from public libraries, museums, art galleries and so on, as well as from the more mundane public services like transport, waste collection and markets. Most towns have a *syndicat d'initiative*, an office which acts as a general coordinating centre for the people of the area, having information about all the cultural activities in the town and surrounding district, about hotels and places of interest to the tourist, and about rooms to let in the town.

c)   Charities

While there are a number of sources of help provided within the State system for people in distress, there is still room for the activities of many charitable organisations. In fact, as previously mentioned, when assessing the circumstances of applicants for social aid, the authorities also take into account any help which might possibly be obtained from unofficial sources. In some *communes* where long-established charities are in operation, the local authorities, rather than provide certain services themselves, simply coordinate and to some extent finance the work of local charities.

GLOSSARY

actifs—working population.
action sanitaire et sociale—financial help given by the *commune* and by the *caisses de sécurité sociale* to people or services in need, as a supplement to statutory awards.
aide—assistance, aid.
aide facultative—discretionary aid (see text).
aide légale—statutory aid (see text).
aide médicale—assistance with medical fees (see text).
allocation—allowance.
allocation d'éducation spécialisée—an allowance paid to parents of children who need special schooling.
allocation des mineurs handicapés—an allowance paid to parents of handicapped children.
allocation spéciale—an allowance paid to old people without any other source of income.
assimilé—someone who, while not technically a paid employee, has the same status for the purposes of the *Sécurité sociale*. (As opposed to *salarié*.)

Association générale des institutions de retraite des cadres (AGIRC)—a complementary pension scheme for salaried staff.

Association des régimes de retraites complémentaires (ARRCO)—an organisation which coordinates complementary pension schemes.

assurance—insurance.

assurance accident du travail—occupational injury insurance.

assurance invalidité—disablement insurance.

assurance maladie—sickness insurance.

assurance maternité—maternity insurance.

assurance vieillesse—pension scheme.

bulletin de soins (bon de docteur)—a voucher issued to recipients of *Aide sociale* which entitles them to one visit to a doctor free of charge.

bureau d'Aide sociale—local office of *Aide sociale*.

Caisse autonome nationale de compensation de l'assurance vieillesse artisanale (CANCAVA)—a pension scheme for self-employed craftsmen.

Caisse régionale d'assurance vieillesse de Strasbourg—a regional pensions office administering the pensions arrangements in the *départements* of Bas-Rhin, Haut-Rhin and Moselle, which are different from those in the rest of France.

condition des ressources—financial means.

congé de maladie—sick leave.

conseil d'administration—management committee (see text).

droits dérivés—rights obtained by virtue of a relationship (e.g. wife, child) to an insured person.

feuille de maladie—a document supplied by the doctor which enables an insured patient to recover all or part of the cost of his treatment.

Fonds national de l'aide au logement—a fund created to assist the aged, young people and the handicapped, by subsidising their accommodation.

Fonds national de l'emploi—a fund created to help businesses to provide employment and to retrain the unemployed.

Fonds national de solidarité—a fund created to provide a supplementary allowance for old people and the disabled.

frais d'accouchement—childbirth expenses.

frais de déplacement—removal expenses, travel expenses.

honoraires—fees.

indemnité forfaitaire—lump sum allowance.

liquidation des pensions—calculation of pensions.

maison de retraite—old people's home.

majoration—increase (in payments).

maladies professionnelles—occupational diseases.

non-salarié—self-employed.

Organisation autonome d'assurance vieillesse de l'industrie et du commerce (ORGANIC)—the pension scheme for self-employed people in industry and commerce.

pension d'ancienneté—retirement pension.

pension de réversion—survivor's (usually widow's) pension.

pension de veuve—widow's pension.

péréquation—the principle whereby pensioners receive a pension assessed according to the current cost of living and salaries, rather than those operating at the time when contributions were paid.

pièce justificative—a document entitling a person to benefit.

plafond—wage ceiling. Contributions by the employee to the *Sécurité sociale* are calculated as 6.45% of the wage below the ceiling plus 1.5% of the full wage.

prestation—benefit.
prestation en espèces—cash benefit.
prestation en nature—benefit in kind.
reclassement—rehabilitation.
régime chapeau—"top-hat scheme". An insurance scheme offered by some employers providing particularly high pensions over and above the compulsory schemes.
salaire de base—basic wage.
salaire de référence—the sum which must be contributed to a pension scheme in order to buy one *point de retraite.*
salarié—employee.
traitement—salary.
travailleur indépendant—self-employed worker.
Union nationale des institutions de retraites des salariés (UNIRS)—the organising body of a complementary pension scheme for employees.

LIST OF ABBREVIATIONS

Abbreviation	Meaning	English term
ACADI	Association des cadres dirigeants de l'industrie	—
AELE	Association européenne de libre-échange	EFTA
AFEI	Association française pour l'étiquetage d'information	—
AFNOR	Association française de normalisation	—
AFP	Association France-presse	—
AFPA	Association pour la formation professionnelle des adultes	—
AGIRC	Association générale des institutions de retraite des cadres	—
AGREF	Association générale des représentants des entreprises françaises	—
AID	Association internationale de développement	IDA
AIEA	Agence internationale de l'énergie atomique	IAEA
AME	Accord monétaire européen	EMA
AMG	Aide médicale gratuite	—
ANAH	Agence nationale pour l'amélioration de l'habitat	—
ANPE	Agence nationale pour l'emploi	—
AP	Assistance publique	—
ARRCO	Association des régimes de retraite complémentaires	—
ASSEDIC	Association pour l'emploi dans l'industrie et le commerce	—
ATIC	Association technique de l'importation charbonnière	—
AVTS	Allocation aux vieux travailleurs salariés	—
BALO	Bulletin des annonces légales obligatoires	—
BAT	Bureau d'assistance technique	TAA
BEI	Banque européenne d'investissements	EIB
BID	Banque interaméricaine de développement	IDB
BIRD	Banque internationale pour la réconstruction et le développement	IBRD
BIT	Bureau international du travail	ILO
BOM	Bureau d'organisation et méthodes	—
BNP	Banque nationale de Paris	—
BRI	Banque des règlements internationaux	BIS
BROCA	Bureau régional d'orientation et de concertation agricoles	—.
BUMIDOM	Bureau pour le développement des migrations intéressant les DOM	—
CAD	Comité d'aide au développement	—
CAECL	Caisse d'aide à l'équipement des collectivités locales	—
CAEM	Conseil d'assistance économique mutuelle	COMECON
CAF	Coût, assurance et frêt	CIF
CANCAVA	Caisse autonome nationale de compensation de l'assurance vieillesse artisanale	—
CAP	Certificat d'aptitude professionnelle	—
CAP	Commission administrative paritaire	—
CAPA	Certificat d'aptitude à la profession d'avocat	—

CAPES	Certificat d'aptitude pédagogique pour l'enseignement secondaire	—
CAR	Commission/conférence administrative régionale	—
CCAG	Cahier des clauses administratives générales	—
CCAP	Cahier des clauses administratives particulières	—
CCBP	Caisse centrale des banques populaires	—
CCDVT	Caisse centrale de dépôts et de virements de titres	—
CCI	Chambre de commerce internationale	ICC
CCM	Commission centrale des marchés	—
CCP	Compte courant/chèque postal	—
CCTG	Cahier des clauses techniques générales	—
CCTP	Cahier des clauses techniques particulières	—
CD	Corps diplomatique	CD
CDC	Caisse des dépôts et consignations	—
CDP	Centre démocratie et progrès	—
CDS	Centre des démocrates sociaux	—
CEA	Centre d'énergie atomique	—
CECA	Communauté européene du charbon et de l'acier	ECSC
CECLES	Centre europén pour la construction de lanceurs d'engins spatiaux	ELDO
CED	Communauté européenne de défense	—
CEE	Commission économique européenne	ECE
CEE	Communauté économique européenne	EEC
CEEA	Communauté européenne de l'énergie atomique (EURATOM)	EAEC (EURATOM)
CEG	Collège d'enseignement général	—
CEJ	Certificat d'études judiciaires	—
CEMT	Conférence européenne des ministres des transports	ECMT
CERES	Centre d'études et de recherches économiques socialistes	—
CERN	Organisation européenne pour la recherche nucléaire	CERN
CES	Collège d'enseignement secondaire	—
CES	Conseil économique et social	—
CET	Collège d'enseignement technique	—
CFDT	Confédération française démocratique du travail	—
CFP	Compagnie française des pétroles	—
CFP	Confédération française des professions	—
CFPC	Centre français du patronat chrétien	—
CFT	Confédération française du travail	—
CFTC	Confédération française des travailleurs chrétiens	—
CGA	Confédération générale de l'agriculture	—
CGC	Confédération générale des cadres	—
CGI	Code général des impôts	—
CGPME	Confédération générale des petites et moyennes entreprises	—
CGT	Compagnie générale transatlantique	—
CGT	Confédération générale du travail	—
CGT-FO	Confédération générale du travail—force ouvrière	—
CICR	Comité international de la Croix rouge	ICRC
CIJ	Cour internationale de justice	ICJ
CJCE	Cour de justice des communautés européennes	CJEC
CJP	Centre des jeunes patrons	—
CLAS	Comité de liaison pour l'autogestion socialiste	—

CNAF	Caisse nationale d'allocations familiales	—
CNAL	Comité national d'action laïque	—
CNAT	Comité national pour l'aménagement du territoire	—
CNAT	Commission nationale pour l'aménagement du territoire	—
CNAV	Caisse nationale d'assurance vieillesse	—
CNC	Comité national de la consommation	—
CNC	Conseil national du commerce	—
CNE	Caisse nationale d'épargne	—
CNER	Conseil national des économies régionales	—
CNES	Centre national des études spatiales	—
CNI	Centre national des indépendants	—
CNIP	Centre national des indépendants et paysans	—
CNME	Caisse nationale des marchés de l'Etat	—
CNPF	Conseil national du patronat français	—
CNR	Compagnie nationale du Rhône	—
CNRS	Centre national de la recherche scientifique	—
CNUCED	Conférence des Nations Unies sur le commerce et le développement	UNCTAD
COB	Commission des opérations de Bourse	—
CODER	Commission de développement économique régional	—
COE	Conseil œcuménique des églises	WCC
COS	Coéfficient d'occupation des sols	—
CPAG	Centre de préparation à l'administration générale	—
CRAM	Caisse régionale d'assurance maladie	—
CROUS	Centre régional des œuvres universitaires et scolaires	—
CRS	Compagnie républicaine de sécurité	—
CVCEP	Commission de vérification des comptes des entreprises publiques	—
DAFU	Direction de l'aménagement foncier et de l'urbanisme	—
DATAR	Délégation à l'aménagement du territoire et à l'action régionale	—
DGI	Direction générale des impôts	—
DOM	Département d'outre-mer	—
DPO	Direction par objectifs	MBO
DRASS	Direction régionale de l'action sanitaire et sociale	—
DST	Direction de la surveillance du territoire	—
DUP	Déclaration d'utilité publique	—
EDF	Electricité de France	—
ENA	Ecole nationale d'administration	—
ENM	Ecole nationale de la magistrature	—
ERAP	Entreprise de recherche et activités pétrolières	—
E-U	Etats-unis	USA
FAS	Fonds d'action sociale	—
FDES	Fonds de développement économique et social	—
FEN	Fédération de l'éducation nationale	—
FENU	Fonds d'équipement des Nations Unies	—
FIAT	Fonds international pour l'aménagement du territoire	—
FISE	Fonds international des Nations Unies pour le secours à l'enfance	UNICEF
FJT	Foyer de jeunes travailleurs	—
FMI	Fonds monétaire international	IMF
FNAFU	Fonds national d'aménagement foncier et d'urbanisme	—
FNAL	Fonds national de l'aide au logement	—

FNOSS	Fédération nationale des organismes de sécurité sociale	—
FNRI	Fédération nationale des républicains indépendants	—
FNS	Fonds national de solidarité	—
FNSEA	Fédération nationale des syndicats d'exploitants agricoles	—
FPA	Formation professionnelle accélérée	—
FSM	Fédération syndicale mondiale	WFTU
FUNU	Force d'urgence des Nations Unies	UNEF
GDF	Gaz de France	—
HLM	Habitation à loyer modéré	—
IDI	Institut de droit international	IIL
IEJ	Institut d'études judiciaires	—
IEP	Institut d'études politiques	—
IFOP	Institut français d'opinion publique	—
IGAME	Inspecteur général de l'administration en mission extraordinaire	—
IGEN	Inspecteur général de l'économie nationale	—
IGF	Inspecteur général des finances	—
INC	Institut national de la consommation	—
INPI	Institut national de la propriété industrielle	—
INSEE	Institut national de la statistique et des études économiques	—
IR	Impôt sur le revenu	—
IRA	Institut régional d'administration	—
IUT	Institut universitaire de technologie	—
JO	Journal officiel	—
JOCE	Journal officiel des communautés européennes	OJEC
MDS	Mouvement démocrate socialiste	—
MJC	Maison des jeunes et de la culture	—
MLF	Mouvement de libération de la femme	—
MRG	Mouvement des radicaux de gauche	—
MRP	Mouvement républicain populaire	—
NF	Norme française	—
OAA	Organisation des Nations Unies pour l'alimentation et l'agriculture	FAO
OACI	Organisation de l'aviation civile internationale	ICAO
OCDE	Organisation de coopération et de développement économique	OECD
OCMI	Organisation consultative maritime intergouvernementale	IMCO
OEA	Organisation des états américains	OAS
OERS	Organisation européenne de recherches spatiales	ESRO
OIC	Organisation internationale du commerce	ITO
OIN	Organisation internationale de normalisation	ISO
OIPC	Organisation internationale de police criminelle (INTERPOL)	ICPO (INTERPOL)
OIT	Organisation internationale du travail	ILO
OMM	Organisation météorologique mondiale	WMO
OMS	Organisation mondiale de la santé	WHO
ONI	Office national d'immigration	—
ONISEP	Office national d'information sur les enseignements et les professions	—
ONU	Organisation des Nations Unies	UNO

ONUDI	Organisation des Nations Unies pour le développement industriel	UNIDO
OP	Ouvrier professionnel	—
OPA	Offre publique d'achat	—
OPEP	Organisation des pays exportateurs de pétrole	OPEC
OREAM	Organisation d'étude d'aménagement de l'aire métropolitaine	—
ORGANIC	Organisation autonome d'assurance vieillesse de l'industrie et du commerce	—
ORSEC	Organisation des secours	—
ORTF	Office de radiodiffusion-télévision française	—
OS	Ouvrier spécialisé	
OTAN	Organisation du traité de l'Atlantique nord	NATO
OTASE	Organisation du traité de l'Asie du sud-est	SEATO
OUA	Organisation de l'unité africaine	OAU
PAZ	Plan d'aménagement de zones	—
PCF	Parti communiste français	—
PEAT	Programme élargi d'assistance technique	—
PEPS	Premier entré, premier sorti	FIFO
PI	Par intérim	acting
PIB	Produit intérieur brut	GDP
PIC	Prêts immobiliers conventionnés	—
PME	Plan de modernisation et d'équipement	—
PMI	Protection maternelle et infantile	—
PMU	Pari mutuel urbain	—
PNB	Produit national brut	GNP
PNUD	Programme des Nations Unies pour le développement	UNDP
PO	Par ordonnance/ordre	—
PS	Parti socialiste	—
PSU	Parti socialiste unifié	—
P et T	Postes et télécommunications	—
RATP	Régie autonome des transports parisiens	—
RCB	Rationalisation des choix budgétaires	PPBS
RDA	République démocratique allemande	GDR
RER	Réseau express régional	—
RFA	République fédérale allemande	FRG
RG	Renseignements généraux	—
RI	Républicains indépendants	—
RN	Revenu national	—
RD	Route départementale	
RPR	Rassemblement pour la République	
RTL	Radio-télé Luxembourg	
SA	Société anonyme	—
SAC	Service d'action civique	—
SAFER	Société d'aménagement foncier et d'établissement rural	—
SARL	Société à responsabilité limité	—
SCI	Société civile immobilière	
SDAU	Schéma directeur d'aménagement et d'urbanisme	
SDECE	Service de documentation extérieure et de contre-espionnage	—
SDN	Société des nations	League of Nations
SDR	Société de développement régional	—

SEITA	Service d'exploitation industrielle des tabacs et allumettes	—
SFI	Société financière internationale	IFC
SFIE	Syndicat des fonctionnaires internationaux et européens	UIECC
SFIO	Section française de l'internationale ouvrière	—
SGF	Statistique général de la France	—
SGF	Statut général des fonctionnaires	—
SICA	Société d'intérêt collectif agricole	—
SICAV	Société d'investissement à capital variable	—
SICOMI	Société immobilière pour le commerce et l'industrie	—
SICOVAM	Société interprofessionnelle pour la compensation des valeurs mobilières	—
SIVOM	Syndicat intercommunal à vocations multiples	—
SJA	Syndicat de la juridiction administrative	—
SMAG	Salaire minimum agricole garanti	—
SMIA	Société mixte d'intérêt agricole	—
SMIC	Salaire minimum de croissance	—
SMIG	Salaire minimum interprofessionnel garanti	—
SNAEN	Syndicat national des agents de l'éducation nationale	—
SNCF	Société nationale de chemins de fer français	—
SNEP	Société nationale des entreprises de presse	—
SNES	Syndicat national de l'enseignement secondaire	—
SNESup	Syndicat national de l'enseignement supérieur	—
SNI	Syndicat national des instituteurs	—
SNIAS	Société nationale industrielle aérospatiale	—
SNPA	Société nationale des pétroles d'Aquitaine	—
SO	Sans observations	—
SOFRES	Société française d'enquête par sondage	—
TAAF	Terres australes et antarctiques françaises	—
TAI	Traitement automatique de l'information	ADP
TC	Taxe complémentaire	—
TEI	Traitement électronique de l'information	EDP
TIR	Transit international routier	TIR
TNP	Théâtre national populaire	—
TOM	Territoire d'outre-mer	—
TVA	Taxe sur la valeur ajoutée	VAT
UCANSS	Union des caisses centrales de mutualité agricole	—
UCCMA	Union des caisses centrales de mutualité agriccie	—
UDCA	Union de défense des commerçants et artisans	—
UDR	Union des démocrates pour la République	—
UEO	Union de l'Europe occidentale	WEU
UEP	Union européenne des paiements	EPU
UER	Unité d'enseignement et de recherche	—
UIMM	Union des industries métallurgiques et minières	—
UIPPI	Union internationale pour la protection de la propriété industrielle (Union de Paris)	IUPIP (Paris Union)
UIT	Union internationale de télécommunications	ITU
UNAF	Union nationale des associations familiales	—
UNCAF	Union nationale des caisses d'allocations familiales	—
UNEDIC	Union nationale des ASSEDIC	—
UNEF	Union nationale des étudiants de France	—
UNIRS	Union nationale des institutions de retraite des salariés	—

UPU	Union postale universelle	UPU
URSS	Union des républiques socialistes soviétiques	USSR
URSSAF	Union pour le recouvrement de la sécurité sociale et des	
	allocations familiales	—
UTA	Union des transports aériens	—
ZAC	Zone d'aménagement concerté	—
ZAD	Zone d'aménagement différé	—
ZAN	Zone d'agglomération nouvelle	—
ZI	Zone industrielle	—
ZUP	Zone à urbaniser par priorité	—

APPENDIX A

Political parties represented in the Parlement (see p. 7)

One feature of a multi-party system, such as that of the French *Parlement*, is that it often leads to difficulties in forming a majority and thus hinders the passing of legislation. As a consequence of this, alliances are frequently formed which may result in the amalgamation of two or more parties with similar views. Equally, in times of political upheaval, splinter groups may break away to form new parties. It is for this reason that the list of political parties has been included as an appendix. It is correct on 1 January 1984 and may be revised at a later date.

Centre national des indépendants et paysans (CNIP)—A party of the right with very conservative policies.

Rassemblement pour la République (RPR)—One of the most powerful parties of the centre-right, formed in 1976 to replace the *Union des démocrates pour la République (UDR)*. It pursues the conservative policies of Gaullism.

Parti républicain—A centre party with liberal tendencies, formed in 1977 to replace the *Fédération nationale des républicains indépendants (FNRI)*. Its policies encourage economic growth and free enterprise.

Centre des démocrates sociaux (CDS)—A party formed in 1977 by the amalgamation of the *Centre démocrate* and the *Mouvement des démocrates sociaux (MDS)*. Its policies are of the social democrat/Christian democrat type.

Parti radical—A long-established party which has moved from a left to a centrist position.

Mouvement des radicaux de gauche (MRG)—Founded in 1971 as a splinter group from the *Parti radical*. It forms part of the presidential majority.

Parti socialiste (PS)—The largest party in France which draws much of its support from the industrial working class. It forms part of the presidential majority.

Parti socialiste unifié (PSU)—A party of the extreme left which advocates workers' control of industry and other socialist policies.

Parti communiste français (PCF)—In recent years the PCF has formed alliances with other left-wing parties in order to present a more united front; it forms part of the presidential majority.

Parliamentary groups (see p. 8)

The number of groups varies from one *Parlement* to another; after the 1981 elections the *députés* were grouped as follows:

> *Groupe du Rassemblement pour la République*
> *Groupe Union pour la Démocratie Française* (consisting of *Parti républicain, Centre des démocrates sociaux,* and *Parti radical*)
> *Groupe socialiste*
> *Groupe communiste*

APPENDIX B

Ministers
(Correct on 1 January 1984)

Ministre de l'intérieur et de la décentralisation—Internal security, police, decentralization matters.
Ministre du commerce extérieur—External trade.
Ministre des transports—Transport.
Ministre du Plan et de l'aménagement du territoire—Matters relating to the "Plan" and to national development.
Ministre de la recherche et de la technologie—Research and technology matters.
Ministre de la solidarité nationale—Social security matters.
Ministre de la justice (also called the *Garde des sceaux*)—Legal matters and law courts.
Ministre des relations extérieures—Foreign affairs.
Ministre des affaires européennes—European Community matters.
Ministre de la défense—Defence.
Ministre de l'économie et des finances—Economic and financial matters.
Ministre de l'éducation nationale—Education.
Ministre de l'agriculture—Agriculture.
Ministre de l'industrie—Industry.
Ministre du commerce et de l'artisanat—Internal trade and small businesses.
Ministre de la culture—Cultural matters.
Ministre du travail—Labour and industrial relations.
Ministre de la santé—Health services.
Ministre du temps libre—Leisure activities.
Ministre de l'urbanisme et du logement—Housing and town-planning.
Ministre de l'environnement—Environmental matters.
Ministre de la mer—Maritime matters.
Ministre de la communication—Media matters.
Ministre des P.T.T.—Post and telecommunication matters.
Ministre des anciens combattants—War pensioners' matters.
Ministre de la consommation—Consumers' protection.
Ministre de la formation professionnelle—Vocational training matters.

INDEX